Consoling the Heart of Jesus

Prayer Companion

From the Do-It-Yourself
Ignatian Retreat

Fr. Michael E. Gaitley, MIC

MARIAN PRESS
STOCKBRIDGE MA 01263

2015

Available from:
Marian Helpers Center
Stockbridge, MA 01263

Prayerline: 1-800-804-3823
Orderline: 1-800-462-7426
www.Marian.org
www.TheDivineMercy.org

Imprimi Potest:
Very Rev. Daniel Cambra, MIC
Provincial Superior
The Blessed Virgin Mary, Mother of Mercy Province
October 5, 2010

ISBN: 978-1-59614-230-5
First edition (5th printing): 2015

Cover Design: Fr. Angelo Casimiro, MIC,
and Kathy Szpak
Page Design: Kathy Szpak
Image, Inside Front Cover: Michael Collopy

Editing and Proofreading: David Came and Andrew Leeco

For texts from the English Edition of *Diary of St. Maria
Faustina Kowalska*

Nihil Obstat:
George H. Pearce, SM
Former Archbishop of Suva, Fiji

Imprimatur:
Joseph F. Maguire
Bishop of Springfield, MA
April 9, 1984

Printed in the United States of America

Consoling the Heart of Jesus

Prayer Companion

From the Do-It-Yourself
Ignatian Retreat

Contents

Preface 9

PART ONE: Laying the Foundation 11
Desire Meditation 13
Consoler Principle and Foundation 16
How Can We Console Jesus if He is Happy
in Heaven? 18

PART TWO: Overcoming Obstacles to Living
the Foundation 23

1. Fear of Suffering 25
Jesus' Words to Joe 25
Deflating the "Second Thing" (Suffering) . . 27
Redemptive Suffering 30

2. Our Weaknesses, Sinfulness, and Attachments . . 31
Weaknesses 32
Sinfulness 34
Attachments 40

3. Fear of Suffering, Again 42
The Best Way to Console Jesus: Trust 42
A Meditation for Consoling Jesus in the
Best Possible Way 43
This Simple and Easy Way Is Powerful 49

4. The Sensitivity of the Lord's Heart 50
A Special Marian Consecration 51
Spiritual Communion of Merciful Love:
Ecce, Fiat, Magnificat 55

5. The Insensitivity of Our Hearts 66
(a) Becoming Sensitive to the Suffering of
Our Neighbor 67

Meditate on the Passion of Christ 67

Examination of Conscience 68

(b) Having Mercy on Our Neighbor in Deed,
    Word, and Prayer 75

Deed: The Merciful Outlook 76

Word: The Merciful Question 79

Prayer: The Chaplet of Divine Mercy and
    Modified "Breathing Prayer" 80

PART THREE: Prayers and Plan of Life 89

A. Prayers 91

1. Divine Mercy Prayers 91

Chaplet of Divine Mercy 91

The Divine Mercy Novena 94

Three O'clock Hour Prayer 105

St. Thérèse's Offering to Merciful Love . . 105
    (short version)

St. Thérèse's Offering to Merciful Love . . 106
    (long version)

Family Offering to Merciful Love and Divine
    Mercy Enthronement 109

2. Prayers of Consecration to Mary 114

Consoler Consecration to Mary 114
    (shorter version)

Consoler Consecration to Mary 115
    (longer version)

St. Louis de Montfort's Consecration
    to Mary 115

St. Maximilian Kolbe's Consecration
    to Mary 116

3. Short Prayers from the *Consoling the Heart of Jesus* Retreat 117

      Yes to Jesus 117

      A Bold Prayer 117

      When My Sin Discourages Me 118

      For Uniting My Will to God's Will 118

      Prayer before a Crucifix 118

      Modified Breathing Prayer "Deal" 119

      Surrender of Worries 119

B. Plan of Life 121

      Consoler Principle and Foundation 121

      A Consoler's Three Promises 122

      A Summary of Trust: *Ecce, Fiat, Magnificat* 123

      Morning Offering 123

      Three Ways to Keep the Three O'clock Hour 124

      Examination of Conscience: B-A-K-E-R . . 126

Preface

This book is a simple guide to living Consoling spirituality. What is Consoling spirituality? One word summarizes it best: *mercy*. To receive mercy from Jesus, to show mercy to one's neighbor, and especially to have mercy on Jesus himself — that's what Consoling spirituality is all about.

Before writing this prayer companion, I published a do-it-yourself retreat that brings a person step-by-step into Consoling spirituality: *Consoling the Heart of Jesus*. This prayer companion goes with it. In fact, I wrote this prayer companion primarily for people who have already made my retreat. I also wrote it as a way of introduction for those who haven't even heard of my retreat, so that they, too, can begin to understand and live Consoling spirituality.

So, what exactly is the *Consoling the Heart of Jesus Prayer Companion*? It's a simple guide to living Consoling spirituality that includes the main ideas, prayers, and meditations of my *Consoling the Heart of Jesus* retreat. In short, it's the whole retreat in summary — though it's not meant to be a substitute for actually making the retreat.

A request from my dear friend, Michele Faehnle, who's a big fan of Consoling spirituality, inspired me to write this prayer companion. One day, she told me, "You know, Fr. Mike, my purse is pretty heavy now, seeing that I'm always lugging around your 430-page book in it. Couldn't you make a little prayer book that has all the essentials of your retreat?"

Michele's request got me thinking, "Hey, I wouldn't mind such a prayer book for myself!" No, I don't have a purse. I thought that because, as life gets busier, I frequently feel the need to get back to my retreat. Problem is, I don't have time to look through the whole book, and I no longer remember where to find specific lessons or prayers when I need them. An easy-to-use summary with the main ideas and prayers well laid out is perfect for me. If you're a hard-core Consoler, then it's probably perfect for you, too.

Hey, Consoler ladies. Say goodbye to annoyingly heavy purses.

Fr. Michael E. Gaitley, MIC, STL

PART ONE

Laying the Foundation

The First Principle and Foundation of Consolers is to become aware of Jesus' suffering and to strive to alleviate it. In Part One, we'll learn about this foundation, which is a consoler's path to sanctity. However, we should first begin with a meditation that will help enkindle in us the desire for holiness.

Desire Meditation

Behold Jesus in front of you, hanging on the Cross. See his gentle, sorrowful face. His Heart aches because so many for whom he's dying have rejected his goodness and love. Will you reject him, too? Before you answer, listen to his words from the Cross, "I thirst." He's speaking to you. He thirsts for you. Do you thirst for him? He thirsts that you might thirst for him. Tell him that you thirst for him. Ask him to help you thirst for him more. Beg him for this grace.

Jesus thirsts for your love, and he wants your help. Will you help him? Before you answer, look at how much he has given you. He created you in love, washed away yours sins in his blood, clothed you with his divine life, and prepares a place in his Father's house for you to dwell with him in joy for all eternity — and there's more. Jesus wants to share with you his mission. He wants your help in bringing everyone back home to his Father. That, too, is his gift to you. Will you accept it? Will you help him? He's counting on your help. He needs you.

Many let Jesus down. They not only refuse his love, but they refuse the gift of the mission he wants to give them. Will you also let him down? Don't worry if you've said no to him in the past. He makes all things new, and his mercy can bring good out of evil. Again, he wants to share his mission with you. Maybe your sharing in it looks different than before; maybe it's exactly the same. No matter. He offers it, and he leads you to it, step-by-step, with his gentle hand. All you need to do is say yes. See how much he loves you, and say yes. Say yes to his love. Believe in his love, and say yes to his will for your life, even if you don't know the details. Remember the gentleness of his face and the sorrow.

If you're having difficulty saying yes to Jesus, turn to Mary. She knows how to say yes to God, and she'll help you. Ask her: "Mary, my mother, please lend me your yes. Please be with me now. Help me not to let Jesus down. Help me to have courage and to believe in his love for me." Ask the angels and your favorite saints to pray for you. Beg the Father and the Holy Spirit to give you a thirst for Jesus, to give you a burning love for the one who burns with love for you.

Now listen to some great news. After having been rejected by so many in our day, Jesus makes it easier than ever before to become a saint. He offers unprecedented graces. In fact, he himself will take charge and make you holy. All you have to do is let him. It won't be too difficult. Trust him. He speaks to you words such as these: "I see your weakness, but be not afraid. Just trust me. I will do it. Let me do it. If only you will trust me and let me do it, I will make you into a saint." Such words remind us of what he said to the great apostle of Divine Mercy, St. Maria Faustina Kowalska: **"Be not afraid of your Savior, O sinful soul. I make the first move to come to you, for I know by yourself you are unable to lift yourself to Me"** (*Diary*, 1485). Such words also remind us of what the saint of the Sacred Heart, Margaret Mary Alacoque, understood so well when she wrote: "His Sacred Heart will do everything for me if I let him. He shall will, he shall love, he shall desire for me and make up for all my faults."

Look again at Jesus, hanging on the Cross. See his gentle, sorrowful face. Hear him say to you, "I thirst." Now earnestly pray: "Jesus, I thirst for you. Help me to thirst for you more. Use me, Jesus. Form me into a saint. Make up for all my faults. I trust in you. With Mary's help, I give you my yes."

Consoler Principle and Foundation

The core of Consoling spirituality is a compassionate response to Jesus in his sorrow. Perhaps nothing reveals the sorrow of Jesus better than the summary statement of his words to St. Margaret Mary, "Behold this Heart which loves so much yet is so little loved." His entire appeal to the saint is as follows. Appearing on the Cross, Jesus said to her in a voice full of sadness and grief:

> There it is, that Heart so deeply in love with men, it spared no means of proof — wearing itself out until it was utterly spent! This meets with scant appreciation from most of them; all I get back is ingratitude — witness their irreverence, their sacrileges, their coldness and contempt for me in this Sacrament of Love. (Cited by Timothy O'Donnell, STD, *Heart of the Redeemer: An Apologia for the Contemporary and Perennial Value of the Devotion to the Sacred Heart of Jesus* [San Francisco: Ignatius Press, 1989], p. 135).

On another occasion, the Lord appeared in front of the exposed Blessed Sacrament with a similar message. Margaret Mary describes the experience:

> Jesus Christ, my kind Master, appeared to me. He was a blaze of glory — his five wounds shining like five suns, flames issuing from all parts of his human form, especially from his divine breast which was like a furnace, and which he opened to disclose his utterly affectionate and loveable Heart, the living source of all those flames. It was at this moment that he revealed to me the indescribable wonders of his pure love for mankind: the extravagance to which he'd been led for those who had nothing for him but ingratitude and indifference. "This hurts me more," he told me, "than everything I suffered in my passion. Even a little love from them in return — and I should regard all that I have done for them as next to nothing, and look for a way of doing still more. But no; all my eager efforts for their welfare meet with nothing but coldness and dislike. Do me the kindness, then — you, at least — of making up for all their ingratitude, as far as you can" (O'Donnell, Ibid., p. 131).

The sorrow of Jesus described in these passages is also captured by his cry from the Cross, "I thirst" — not a thirst for water but a thirst for love. This appeal for love gets to the heart of a consoler's relationship with Jesus, because by hearing his cry, a consoler responds by striving to quench his thirst.

How Can We Console Jesus if He is Happy in Heaven?

We can only console people who are suffering. But isn't Jesus happy in heaven? Well, if he's happy in heaven, then we can't really speak of consoling him except in the sense that we can console the suffering members of his Body. Right? Wrong. We can also give consolation to Jesus, the sorrowful Head of the Body. We can do this "retroactively," which means we can console him now for his suffering during his earthly life. How this is so, is described by Pope Pius XI in his encyclical letter on the Sacred Heart of Jesus, *Miserentissimus Redemptor*. Reflecting on Jesus' agony in the Garden, the Pope writes:

> Now if, because of our sins also which were as yet in the future, but were *foreseen*, the soul of Christ became sorrowful unto death, it

cannot be doubted that then, too, already He derived somewhat of solace from our reparation, which was *likewise foreseen*, when "there appeared to him an angel from heaven" (Lk 22:43), in order that His Heart, oppressed with weariness and anguish, might find consolation. And so even now, in a wondrous yet true manner, *we can and ought to console that Most Sacred Heart which is continually wounded by the sins of thankless men*, since — as we also read in the sacred liturgy — Christ Himself, by the mouth of the Psalmist complains that He is forsaken by His friends: "My Heart hath expected reproach and misery, and I looked for one that would grieve together with me, but there was none: and for one that would comfort me, and I found none" (Ps 69:21) (emphasis added; 13).

It seems that we might also give consolation to Jesus in a sense that is captured in the following passage by the early Church Father Origen:

My Saviour grieves even now about my sins. My Saviour cannot rejoice as long as I remain in perversion. Why cannot he do this? Because he himself is "an intercessor for our sins with the Father." ... How can he, who is an intercessor for my sins, drink the "wine" of joy, when I grieve him with my sins? How can he, who "approaches the altar" in order to atone for me a sinner, be joyful when the sadness of sin rises up to him ceaselessly? "With you," he says, "I will drink in the Kingdom of my Father." As long as we do not act in such a way that we can mount up to the Kingdom, he cannot drink alone that wine which he promised to drink with us. ... Thus it is that he waits until we should be converted, in order that we may follow in his footsteps and he rejoice "with us" and "drink wine with us in the Kingdom of his Father." ... We are the ones who delay his joy by our negligence toward our lives.

... [But] the apostles too have not yet received their joy: they likewise are waiting for me to participate in their joy. So it is that the saints who depart from here do not immediately receive the full reward of their merits, but wait for us, even if we delay, even if we remain sluggish. They cannot know perfect joy as long as they grieve over our transgressions and weep for our sins.

... You will have joy when you depart from this life if you are a saint. But your joy will be complete only when no member of your body is lacking to you. For you too will wait, just as you are awaited. But if you, who are a member, do not have perfect joy as long as a member is missing, how much more must our Lord and Saviour, who is the head and origin of this body, consider it an incomplete joy if he is still lacking certain of his members? ... Thus he does not want to receive his perfect glory without you: that means, not without his people which is "his body" and "his members" (*In Lev. Hom.* 7, 2, cited by Josef Ratzinger in *Eschatology: Death and Eternal Life*, trans. Michael Waldstein, ed. Aidan Nichols, OP (Washington, DC: The Catholic University of America Press, 1988), p. 185-186).

Although Cardinal Josef Ratzinger (the future Pope Benedict XVI) thought there were some problems with the mythological expression of this passage, he believed that it best captures an important truth about the relation between human life, history, and love. Developing this insight, he writes that love is such that it's always *for* someone. He then applies this idea to the love the saints in heaven have for those who are still suffering on earth:

> Love cannot, then, close itself against others or be without them so long as time, and with it suffering, is real. No one has formulated this insight more finely than Thérèse of Lisieux with her idea of heaven as the showering down of love towards all. But even in ordinary human terms we can say, "How could a mother be completely and unreservedly happy so long as one of her children is suffering?" (Ibid., 188).

That last line gets to the heart of it. How could Jesus Christ, who loves us with an even greater love than that of a mother, be completely happy in heaven while the members of his body are suffering? It seems he can't be. This side of eternity, we can't fully understand exactly how it is that he suffers with us, but he does, and furthermore, he desires our consoling love.

PART TWO

Overcoming Obstacles to Living the Foundation

1. FEAR OF SUFFERING

Our principle and foundation is to console the Heart of Jesus, which is so sorrowful. But isn't this idea of consoling the Heart of Jesus the same as making reparation to his Sacred Heart? And isn't reparation full of painful penances and difficult spiritual disciplines? Well, then, this idea of bearing extra suffering for Christ may begin to pull us away from the idea of consoling Jesus.

Don't worry. We'll overcome this obstacle by coming to know the Lord's gentleness (see Jesus' words to Joe that follow) and by coming to know the true meaning of suffering.

Jesus' Words to Joe

On the very last day of his 30-day Ignatian retreat, during one of the last meditations of the retreat, a young man named Joe was having a kind of crisis. The instructions for the meditation directed him to beg the Lord Jesus for an intimate knowledge of all the blessings he'd received in his life. Joe, who had been greatly blessed, was terrified to do this as he thought to himself, "Those to whom much is given, much is expected" (see Lk 12:48). Then, he became paralyzed with fear as he wondered what God would demand of him in return. Surely, his bloody crucifixion! Just then, the Lord spoke more clearly to Joe than he ever had up to that point. In sad but gentle and loving words, Jesus said:

> "Joseph, Joseph, why are you hesitating? Why do you fear?"

> Joe responded, "Lord, if I look at all you've given me, I'm terrified of what you might want in return."

> The Lord continued: "Joseph, haven't I shown you how gentle I am with you? Haven't I shown you only kindness? Why do you fear? Look at your life. Have I ever allowed anything you couldn't bear?"

> Joe had to admit, "No, Lord, all you've shown me is mercy and love, and the tough times came when I went off on my own."

> Then, the Lord began, "Joseph, all I want ..."

> He had all of Joe's (nervous) attention, "Yes, Lord?"

> "All I want is for you to be my friend. All I want is for you not to be afraid of me and to come to me."

> "That's all, Lord?"

> "That's all."

After this conversation, Joe's heart over-flowed with peace. Perhaps peace is beginning to fill our hearts as well. For the Lord's words to Joe are addressed to all little souls: "All I want is for you to be my friend. All I want is for you not to be afraid of me and to come to me. That's all." Can you hear the Lord speaking these words to you? He does. Listen with your heart. You don't have to make a 30-day retreat to hear them. Here they are, right now, for you. Take them to heart, and realize how simple it is to please the Lord.

Deflating the "Second Thing" (Suffering)

Our Principle and Foundation is to console the Heart of Jesus. That's the "first thing." However, there's a danger that "second things" might distract us from the "first thing." One of the second things that easily distracts people is suffering. Knowing this, the devil often inflates this second thing so much that it becomes larger than life, frightens us, and blocks our view of the "first thing," namely, Jesus. My aim here is to deflate suffering down to its true size, so we'll see it's not so scary. In fact, once it's deflated, we might even begin to find in suffering a source of joy — but let's not get ahead of ourselves. Let's start by dispelling a big misconception about suffering.

People often think they can escape suffering. They can't. Suffering finds us all. Everyone in the world suffers: rich and poor, healthy and sick, young and old. It might not always look like certain people suffer, but suffering comes in various forms, many of which are hidden. Truly, if we look back on our own lives, we find at least some confirmation of the idea that suffering is part of the human condition.

While we may know that suffering is an inevitable aspect of life, there's at least a small part of us that silently rebels against this fact and spends a lot of time and energy trying to find ways to avoid it. Like suffering itself, this part of us is a simple fact of life. That being said, we don't have to let it control our lives. Indeed, we should resist that temptation. For, again, suffering finds us all, no matter how much we strive to avoid it, and those who make such striving the center of their lives often end up being the ones who suffer the most.

The best way to deal with suffering is to accept it, unite it to Christ in his suffering, and begin to find its hidden treasure. By accepting suffering, I don't mean we should be completely passive such that we don't act to avoid the suffering of poverty, illness, and the like — the part of us that strives to avoid suffering has a legitimate role in our lives. So what do I mean by accepting suffering? To explain this idea, it'll be helpful to contrast it with something else.

It seems to me there are at least two different Christian approaches to suffering. The first approach (the approach of big souls) tends to be very active. It involves actively choosing lots of penances, mortifications, and sacrifices. Such an approach has a long history in the Church and has helped produce a number of saints. It's not what I'll be emphasizing here. Consoling spirituality is for little souls, and the approach to suffering that follows is for them.

I propose a more passive approach to suffering that's in keeping with the theme of "letting Jesus do it." In other words, I propose that we first ask Jesus to choose for us the suffering that he knows will form us into saints (for he knows best) and then simply accept what he sends. If you're worried that it won't be enough, that he won't really find crosses for you, that he'll forget — don't. I can only say from experience, there's no need to worry. He won't forget. Yet maybe that's not the problem. Maybe you're not worried that Jesus will forget to find crosses for you. Maybe you're worried that he'll remember and that the crosses he'll choose will be too heavy. I will again say from experience, don't worry. Jesus is amazingly gentle. He knows what we can take and what we need. In fact, you might even come to find, as I have, that he's gentler with us than we are with ourselves.

Redemptive Suffering

In his great goodness and mercy, Jesus allows us to participate in his redeeming action in the world. In fact, he needs us. In a very real sense, he needs our suffering to be united with his in order to save souls. We can begin to understand this mystery if we reflect on some puzzling words of St. Paul: "I rejoice in my sufferings for your sake, and in my flesh I complete what is lacking in the suffering of Christ for the sake of his body, the Church ..." (Col 1:24). How can St. Paul write that there's something "lacking" in the suffering of Christ? Jesus' suffering is objectively enough to save everyone, and the graces his suffering merits are available to all. In this sense, there's absolutely nothing lacking in his suffering. Yet there's a kind of "lack" in Christ's suffering in the sense that not everyone subjectively accepts his grace and mercy. Moreover, there's also a lack in his suffering when people don't *fully* accept his grace and mercy, that is, when they do so halfheartedly and with reservations and conditions. It's precisely in such situations where people reject or don't fully accept God's grace that our sufferings and bold prayers can come in to "complete what is lacking."

There's a mysterious respect the Lord has for human free will. He will not (and cannot) force us to choose him and love him. Yet, when we use our free will on behalf of others, we somehow can influence the free will of those other people. How this happens, we don't know. Still, because of this influence we can have on one another, Jesus and Mary constantly plead with us to pray and to offer up our sufferings, especially for unrepentant sinners. Think, for instance, of Our Lady of Fatima who was so sad because, as she said to the shepherd children, many souls go to hell because no one prays and offers up suffering for them. Or think of our Lord's sobering words to St. Faustina, **"Be assured that the grace of eternal salvation for certain souls in their final moment depends on your prayer"** (*Diary*, 1777).

2. OUR WEAKNESSES, SINFULNESS, AND ATTACHMENTS

Our weaknesses, sinfulness, and attachments can make us afraid to go to the Lord. We may think, "I can't go to Jesus because I'm such a spiritual mess." This is a lie. Jesus' merciful Heart is most attracted to weak, sinful souls, and he raises them up if only they'll let him. Now let's consider how our weaknesses, sinfulness, and attachments can be seen not as obstacles to holi-

ness but ways that lead us to greater reliance on the Lord and his mercy.

Weaknesses

Do you believe that it's impossible for you to become a saint? Do you feel too full of weaknesses? So did St. Thérèse of Lisieux's sister, Marie — at first. Then Thérèse taught her otherwise.

Marie had written to Thérèse, saying that it seemed impossible for her to love God like Thérèse loved him. Thérèse responded to her sister's discouragement with one of the most beautiful letters ever written:

> Dear Sister, … How can you ask me if it is possible for you to love God as I love Him? …
>
> If you had understood the story of my little bird, you would not have asked me this question. My [_____ (fill in the blank: virtues, talents, many gifts, etc.)] *are nothing*, they are not what give me the unlimited confidence that I feel in my heart. They are, to tell the truth, the spiritual riches that *render one unjust*, when one rests in them with complacence and when one believes they are

something great. ... Ah! I really feel that it is not this at all that pleases God in my little soul; what pleases Him is that *He sees me loving my littleness and my poverty, the blind hope that I have in His mercy.* ... That is my only treasure. ... [W]hy would this treasure not be yours?

... Oh, dear Sister, I beg you, understand your little girl, understand that to love Jesus, to be His *victim of love*, the weaker one is, without desires or virtues, the more suited one is for the workings of this consuming and transforming Love. ... [B]ut we must consent to remain always poor and without strength, and this is the difficulty ... . Ah! let us remain then *very far* from all that sparkles, let us love our littleness, let us love to feel nothing, then we shall be poor in spirit, and Jesus will come to look for us [and] He will transform us in flames of love.

... Oh! how I would like to be able to make you understand what I feel! ... It is confidence and nothing but confidence that must lead us to Love (emphasis in original; Letter 197 to Sr. Marie of the Sacred

Heart, September 17, 1896. *Letters of St. Thérèse of Lisieux*, vol. II, 1890-1897, trans. John Clarke, OCD [Washington, DC: ICS Publications, 1982], p. 998).

Sinfulness

The logic is simple, though we often forget it. Jesus is infinite mercy, and his merciful Heart is most attracted to weak, sinful souls. Therefore, when sinners repent of their sins and turn to him, it gives him great joy and consolation. Scripture attests to this, "There is more joy in heaven over one sinner who repents than over ninety-nine righteous persons who need no repentance" (Lk 15:7). The *Diary of St. Faustina* is also full of testimony to this. Here are some examples that we'd do well to prayerfully consider when our sinfulness tempts us to avoid the Lord Jesus. (The words in boldface type are Jesus' words to St. Faustina. The words without boldface type are Faustina's words.)

I desire trust from My creatures. Encourage souls to place great trust in My fathomless mercy. Let the weak, sinful soul have no fear to approach Me, for even if it had more sins than there are grains of sand in the world, all would be drowned in the unmeasurable depths of My mercy (1059).

[Let] the greatest sinners place their trust in My mercy. They have the right before others to trust in the abyss of My mercy. My daughter, write about My mercy toward tormented souls. Souls that make an appeal to My mercy delight Me. To such souls I grant even more graces than they ask. I cannot punish even the greatest sinner if he makes an appeal to My compassion, but on the contrary, I justify him in My unfathomable and inscrutable mercy. Write: before I come as a just Judge, I first open wide the door of My mercy. He who refuses to pass through the door of My mercy must pass through the door of My justice (1146).

My daughter, write that the greater the misery of a soul, the greater its right to My mercy; [urge] all souls to trust in the unfathomable abyss of My mercy, because I want to save them all. On the cross, the fountain of My mercy was opened wide by the lance for all souls — no one have I excluded! (1182)

My Secretary, write that I am more generous toward sinners than toward the just. It was for their sake that I came down from heaven; it was for their sake that My Blood was spilled. Let them not fear to approach Me; they are most in need of My mercy (1275).

Be not afraid of your Savior, O sinful soul. I make the first move to come to you, for I know that by yourself you are unable to lift yourself to Me. Child, do not run away from your Father; be willing to talk openly with your God of mercy who wants to speak words of pardon and lavish His graces on you. How dear your soul is to Me! I have inscribed your name upon My hand; you are engraved as a deep wound in My Heart (1485).

My mercy is greater than your sins and those of the entire world. Who can measure the extent of My goodness? For you I descended from heaven to earth; for you I allowed Myself to be nailed to the cross; for you I let My Sacred Heart be pierced with a lance, thus opening wide the source of mercy for you. Come, then, with trust to draw graces from this fountain. I never reject a contrite heart. Your misery has disappeared in the depths of My mercy. Do not argue with Me about your wretchedness. You will give Me pleasure if you hand over to Me all your troubles and griefs. I shall heap upon you the treasures of My grace (1485).

O soul steeped in darkness, do not despair. All is not yet lost. Come and confide in your God, who is love and mercy (1486).

What joy fills My Heart when you return to Me. Because you are weak, I take you in My arms and carry you to the home of My Father (1486).

You see, My child, what you are of yourself. The cause of your falls is that you rely too much upon yourself and too little on Me. But let this not sadden you so much. You are dealing with the God of mercy, which your misery cannot exhaust. Remember, I did not allot only a certain number of pardons (1488).

Do not lose heart in coming for pardon, for I am always ready to forgive you (1488).

All grace flows from mercy, and the last hour abounds with mercy for us. Let no one doubt concerning the goodness of God; even if a person's sins were as dark as night, God's mercy is stronger than our misery. One thing alone is necessary: that the sinner set ajar the door of his heart, be it ever so little, to let in a ray of God's merciful grace, and then God will do the rest. But poor is the soul who has shut the door on God's mercy, even at the last hour. It was just such souls who plunged Jesus into deadly sorrow in the Garden of Olives (1507).

Write this for the benefit of distressed souls: when a soul sees and realizes the gravity of

its sins, when the whole abyss of the misery into which it immersed itself is displayed before its eyes, let it not despair, but with trust let it throw itself into the arms of My mercy, as a child into the arms of its beloved mother. These souls have a right of priority to My compassionate Heart, they have first access to My mercy. Tell them that no soul that has called upon My mercy has been disappointed or brought to shame. I delight particularly in a soul which has placed its trust in My goodness (1541).

Even if I had had the sins of the whole world, as well as the sins of all the condemned souls weighing on my conscience, I would not have doubted God's goodness but, without hesitation, would have thrown myself into the abyss of the divine mercy, which is always open to us; and, with a heart crushed to dust, I would have cast myself at His feet, abandoning myself totally to His holy will, which is mercy itself (1552).

O soul, whoever you may be in this world,
Even if your sins were as black as night,
Do not fear God, weak child that you are,
For great is the power of God's mercy (1652).

You see My mercy for sinners, which at this moment is revealing itself in all its power. See how little you have written about it; it is

only a single drop. Do what is in your power, so that sinners may come to know My goodness (1665).

There are souls who thwart My efforts, but I have not given up on them; as often as they turn to Me, I hurry to their aid, shielding them with My mercy, and I give them the first place in My compassionate Heart (1682).

O God of compassion, You alone can justify me, and You will never reject me when I, contrite, approach Your Merciful Heart, where no one has ever been refused, even if he were the greatest sinner (1730).

Write, My daughter, that I am mercy itself for the contrite soul. A soul's greatest wretchedness does not enkindle Me with wrath; but rather, My Heart is moved toward it with great mercy (1739).

I am mercy itself; therefore I ask you to offer Me your misery and this very helplessness of yours and, in this way, you will delight My Heart (1775).

How very much I desire the salvation of souls! My dearest secretary, write that I want to pour out My divine life into human souls and sanctify them, if only they were willing

to accept My grace. The greatest sinners would achieve great sanctity, if only they would trust in My mercy (1784).

Attachments

There's a gentle way that the Lord frees little souls from their attachments. Allow me to explain with the following illustration.

Have you ever played fetch with a dog? You throw a ball and the dog retrieves it. Sometimes when the dog returns, however, it doesn't drop the ball. "Drop it," you say, but the dog doesn't drop it. You try grabbing the ball from the dog's mouth, but it doesn't let go and maybe even growls. If this happens, what do you do? Here's a suggestion. If the dog won't drop the ball, try getting down there with it. Pet it real nicely and say, "Nice doggie … that's a *good* dog." As it begins to wag its tail and relax, grasp the ball without the dog noticing, and pull it out with a quick and easy jerk. It works like a charm. Well, that's sometimes how the Lord deals with us. Sound strange? Allow me to explain.

When we go to Jesus, especially to his Real Presence in the Blessed Sacrament, he fills us with his love and peace, and at the same time, in his great mercy, he silently loosens our grip on our attachments. After some time, without us realizing it, he holds what he's just pulled out of our mouths. There it is in his beautiful hands, or rather, there it is as it's burning up in the flames of his merciful Heart: that dirty, old ball covered with spit! The moral, of course, is to trust the Lord, to go to him. He'll help us become detached, and it'll happen with a certain ease.

Yes, trust the Lord. Go to him as you are with all your attachments, and don't worry. With some things he'll say, "No, you're not ready to get rid of that, but please just sit here with me and console my Heart, which hurts so much." At other times, as you're sitting there before him, clinging to something very tightly, he just might begin by saying, "Nice doggie … ." But again, don't worry. Be completely honest about your deepest attachments. You can even say, "Lord, you *know* I'm not ready to let go of this … but if you want, you can change my desire for it." That's not a cop out. In fact, Jesus made a similar prayer in the Garden of Gethsemane, "My Father, if it be possible, let this cup pass away from me; yet not as I will, but as thou wilt" (Mt 26:39). So, trust him. Don't be afraid to stand before his gaze of love. If any surgery is needed, know that if we stay fixed on him, it's virtually painless.

3. FEAR OF SUFFERING, AGAIN

As our love for Jesus grows, we'll want to console him more and more, even in the best possible way. However, a fear may accompany these desires, namely, the fear that consoling Jesus in the "best possible way" will lead to lots of suffering. Don't worry. Remember that the Lord is very gentle with little souls, and the best possible way to console him is not so difficult after all.

The Best Way to Console Jesus: Trust

What hurts the Lord's heart most? Lack of trust. It's when those who are closest to him don't trust him. Well, what consoles Jesus the most? Trust. But what does trust mean? How does one live trust? One lives trust by praise and thanksgiving, by praising and thanking God in all things and for everything. Thus, when good things come our way (by good things, I mean what makes it easy to give praise and thanks), we strive to praise and thank God for them. For instance, on a given day, we might praise and thank God for a good meal with family and friends, beautiful music, or a wonderful scene of nature. Then, when God sends (or permits) those things that often make it difficult to praise and thank him (crosses), we strive to praise and thank him for them, too. Now, let's do a meditation that aims to console Jesus with our trust.

A Meditation for Consoling Jesus in the Best Possible Way

We're at the bottom of the hill of Calvary, also known as Golgotha. Look up the hill. See Jesus at the top, hanging on the Cross. He doesn't see us because he's surrounded by a huge crowd of people.

The people who surround the Cross laugh at Jesus. They mock him and insult him right to his face. They aren't afraid to go to him. No, they go right up to him, laughing and even spitting at him. The Lord loves them, but his Heart is broken because of their rejection, which means their own death if they don't change, for he is Life.

Many dark shadows go in and out of the crowd. They're demons. They enjoy stirring up the crowd to mock and torture Jesus more. Seeing us at the bottom of the hill, two of them approach. The first one stands about seven feet tall, and his face is a featureless void. He stops directly in front of you. As he towers over you, he says in a terrible, hissing voice, "You jussst ssstay right where you are and everything will be jussst fine." Meanwhile, the other demon, a ghost-like little creature no bigger than a sparrow, settles on your shoulder and whispers in your ear:

> You don't belong here. Don't you have other things to do? You don't need to be here. This is much too painful for you to see. After all, aren't you the reason for that man's torture? Don't you have some important business to take care of? Isn't that television show you like so much going to start soon? Go ahead. Go take your mind off this. There's nothing you can do. Look at the huge crowd. What difference is your being here going to make?

These words are tempting. Thoughts come into your mind: "Yes, what am I among so many? Jesus won't notice if I go home. He'll never even know I was here. Besides, it's cold, and he'll probably be dead soon anyway."

So there you are at the bottom of the hill. The crowd is overwhelming. These demons are frightening. You're a sinner aren't you? Perhaps you've lost your right to be here since you've sinned so much, and really, what can one person do amid such a multitude of people? Standing here, hesitating, you're stuck at the bottom of the hill. Meanwhile, Jesus suffers alone.

What was that? Did you hear it? What's such a beautiful sound doing amid so much blasphemy and raucous laughter? It's a woman's voice. Sweetly, it begins to fill your soul, bringing it light and peace:

> Listen and put it into your heart, my dear little child. The thing that frightens you, the thing that afflicts you, is nothing. Do not let it disturb you. Am I not here who am your Mother? Are you not under my care and protection? Am I not the source of your joy? Are you not in the hollow of my mantle, in the crossing of my arms. Do you need something more? Let nothing else worry you or disturb you.

Mary is with us. Let's go with confidence to the foot of the Cross. Let's run there. Nothing can harm us. Mary is with us! She'll teach us what to do. Let's go console Jesus with Mary.

Filled with courage, we run up the hill. Demons scream in horror as they're cast aside by some invisible force. One cries out, "No! Don't let them! Everything will be ruined!" The ugly mob parts like the Red Sea, and some are struck dumb. We arrive at the foot of the Cross. Look up. Behold that Heart which loves so much yet is so little loved. Unfortunately, Jesus still doesn't see us. His sorrowful gaze is on the crowd.

Turn now to Mary. Speak to her from your helplessness: "Mary, what can I do? I'm so weak, and I, too, have hurt Jesus and caused this."

Smiling, despite her tears, she tenderly speaks to you:

> Just tell him. Tell my Son that you love him. Thank him for what he is suffering right now out of love for you. Smile at him. Give him what you can. Here, I will help you. I will hold you up to him.

Mary takes you into her arms and lifts you close to the broken face of the Savior. He seems dazed and still doesn't see you — he only sees the rejection of the crowd. You touch his cheek with your hand and direct his face toward yours. Now he sees you. You smile and speak to him from your heart:

> Lord, don't look at them. Look at me. ... Lord Jesus, even though my sins are many, I know the mercy of your Heart. I'm sorry I was afraid to go to you. I'm so sorry I left you alone. But look, here I am. Please forgive me my sins. I'm going to try

to do better. Please forgive the sins of those in the crowd, too. Lord, if only they knew you, they'd love you.

Lord, I can't offer much right now except for my weak trust and love. Jesus, I do trust in you, and I love you. I praise you, Jesus, and thank you for everything, especially for what you're suffering right now out of love for me. I've come to be with you, my friend. Don't be sad. I love you, and there's nowhere else I'd rather be than right here, praising you, thanking you, and consoling your broken Heart.

As you go on in this way, even singing your praise and thanks to Jesus, Mary joins her voice with yours.

These acts of love take the Lord by surprise. He was longing for love, and he's found a return. The demons are howling and grinding their teeth, but they're a million miles away. In this one moment, as you come to Jesus as you are, you distract him from all the abuse, rejection, and sin that his Sacred Heart is always enduring.

Of course, Jesus still feels the pain of rejection and sin, but as he looks from the Cross and sees your confident love, you really do distract him from the circus of abuse that surrounds him. Suddenly, he says to you, "My beloved friend, seeing your great confidence and love, I wish I could suffer even more." Yes, seeing you here, loving him and thanking him, makes it all worth it to him. This is what he's been waiting and hoping for. Now his suffering is somehow relieved, and he continues speaking to you: "Child, you are a delight to my Heart. At last, I have found some rest. My friend, I have found rest in your heart. Thank you for being with me at this hour."

Hearing such words from the Lord is the greatest joy for those who have dedicated themselves to consoling him — and we can be assured that Jesus always speaks such words to us whenever we go to him with confidence. Let us be convinced that our little acts of love and trust give delight to Jesus. We may not always be able to hear him saying so, but we can believe that he does take delight in them. If we do believe it, then going to the Lord is a constant joy.

May we find this joy always as we visit Jesus and carry him in our hearts. May we also realize just how powerful our going to the Lord with joyful trust really is. It may seem like a little thing, but it amounts to a lot.

This Simple and Easy Way Is Powerful

In the meditation we just made, we may have come to realize that just one person full of trust can, in a sense, make Jesus forget about all the abuse he receives from the world at a certain time. As St. Faustina wrote, such a person becomes a "mist" before the eyes of Jesus that blocks from his view the terrible sins of the world (*Diary*, 284).

Do we realize the power of this? If we simply live with an attitude of trust, if we go to Jesus full of confidence, then each of us can make him forget about the rejection he continually receives. Yes, he'll still feel the pain caused by humanity's sins, but it'll be like nothing to him, for, from the Cross, he'll say to us those remarkable words we heard earlier, "I wish I could suffer even more." He says this. He'll say it to you. Listen with your heart.

By the way, if we're worried that by focusing on Jesus and consoling him we might be neglecting the other people and projects we should be praying for, realize this: Jesus is not outdone in generosity. If we make efforts to console him, he'll take care of the rest. As he said to one mystic, Sr. Consolata Betrone, "You, worry only about loving me, and I will take care of everything else to the smallest detail." Yes. That's it. Focusing on consoling Jesus is not a waste of time or prayer. If we stay fixed on our goal, he'll take care of all our cares, all those who are dear to us, and much more than we can imagine. Yes, our efforts to console Jesus cause love and grace to multiply and flow out to the whole world — and it's so easy to do. We can focus on him by visiting him in the Most Blessed Sacrament or simply by being mindful of his true presence in our hearts through grace, even as we do things like mopping the floor or mowing the lawn. So what's stopping us from doing this most important work, even in the midst of our work? Truly, it can change the world.

So, let's fly past the demons and the miserable crowd and go straight to the foot of the Cross to console our Lord. As we begin, a little devil puts up yet another obstacle to trip us on our way.

4. THE SENSITIVITY OF THE LORD'S HEART

The Heart of Jesus is very sensitive, which makes for some good news and some bad news. The good news is that it's relatively easy to console the Lord's Heart in the best way: It simply takes our trust! The bad news is that it's also relatively easy to break the Lord's Heart in the worst way: It simply takes our lack of trust. For those whose principle and foundation is to console the Heart of Jesus, this bad news is deeply troubling. But thank goodness Jesus taught our friend Joe that there are two ways by which we can be assured that we won't deeply wound the Lord by our lack of trust: A Special Marian Consecration and a Spiritual Communion of Merciful Love.

A Special Marian Consecration

Marian consecration basically means giving Mary our full permission (or as much permission as we can) to complete her motherly task in us, which is to form us into other Christs. Thus, by consecrating ourselves to Mary, each of us is saying to her:

> Mary, I want to be a saint. I know that you also want me to be a saint and that it's your God-given mission to form me into one. So, Mary, at this moment, on this day, I freely choose to give you my full permission to do your work in me, with your Spouse, the Holy Spirit.

As soon as Mary hears us make such a decision, she flies to us and begins working a masterpiece of grace within our souls. She continues this work for as long as we don't deliberately choose to change our choice from a yes to a no, as long as we don't take back our permission and leave her. That being said, it's always a good idea for us to strive to deepen our "yes" to Mary. For the deeper our "yes" becomes, the more marvelously she can perform her works of grace in our souls.

One of the greatest aspects of being consecrated to Mary is that she's such a gentle mother. She makes the lessons of the Cross into something sweet, and she pours her motherly love and solace into our every wound. Going to her and giving her permission to do her job truly is the "surest, easiest, shortest and the most perfect means" to becoming a saint. What joy it is to be consecrated to Jesus through Mary!

Now, having learned what Marian consecration is, we can appreciate a special emphasis Joe gave to his consecration to Jesus through Mary during his retreat. Feeling moved by the Holy Spirit, he prayed the following:

> Today I renew my total consecration to you, Mary, my mother. I give you my whole being so you may lead me to console your Son with the perfect consolation you give to him. From this day forward, dear Jesus, whenever I embrace you, may it be with the arms of Mary. Whenever I kiss you, may it

be with the lips of Mary. Whenever I sing to you, praise you, and thank you, may it be with the voice of Mary. Jesus, in short, every time I love you, may it be with the Heart of Mary.

We see in this prayer that Joe gave Mary his yes with a particular emphasis: He gave her permission to be with him in a special way in his mission of consoling Jesus. Still, why would Jesus teach this consecration to Joe as a way of being assured that he would always be a consolation to his Heart? More specifically, why would Jesus say that this consecration prevents Joe from wounding his Heart with distrust? Well, look at it this way: When we console Jesus with the Heart of Mary, our acts of trust and love go to Jesus through the perfect faith and love of his mother. Thus, even if our acts of trust are not so perfect — even if they're tainted with some distrust — they don't hurt Jesus, because Mary's faith makes up for what we lack.

To help us understand better something of the mystery of how Mary can make up for our lack, it might be helpful to meditate on a passage from *True Devotion to Mary* by St. Louis de Montfort. In the context of explaining how Mary embellishes and adorns everything we give to Jesus, de Montfort writes:

It is as if a peasant, wishing to gain the friendship and benevolence of the king, went to the queen and presented her with a fruit which was his whole revenue, in order that she might present it to the king. The queen, having accepted the poor little offering from the peasant, would place the fruit on a large and beautiful dish of gold, and so, on the peasant's behalf, would present it to the king. Then the fruit, however unworthy in itself to be a king's present, would become worthy of his majesty because of the dish of gold on which it rested and the person who presented it (*True Devotion to Mary*, trans. Frederick W. Faber [Charlotte, NC: TAN Books, 1941], p. 93).

So, when we at least try to console Jesus with our trust (even if our whole bodies shake with anxiety), when we at least try to be full of praise and thanks (even if we look gloomy and sad), and when we at least try to remain with our friend (even if our minds are distracted by 1,000 different things), then we don't need to fear hurting our Lord. He sees that we want to console him, and because his mother makes up for what we lack (if we're consecrated to her), we always do console him as long as we keep trying. We ought to ponder this reality, for it's a truly great gift.

Spiritual Communion of Merciful Love: *Ecce, Fiat, Magnificat*

The second way that prevents us from deeply wounding the Lord by our lack of trust is by making and living the Spiritual Communion of Merciful Love. To begin, we first need to know what the Offering to Merciful Love is.

What's the Offering to Merciful Love? It's basically this. First, it's to see, like St. Thérèse saw, that the Heart of Jesus is sorrowful because so many people reject his merciful love. Then, for the purpose of consoling Jesus, it's to give him permission to fill us with all the mercy others have rejected. He surely does fill us if we give him permission, and this gives him great relief primarily because someone has chosen to receive his mercy fully and secondarily because the mercy that fills such a soul begins to overflow to others. At its core, the Offering to Merciful Love is simply to receive Jesus' rejected mercy. Words the Lord spoke to St. Faustina express well this essence of the offering:

My Heart overflows with great mercy for souls, and especially for

poor sinners. ... I desire to bestow My graces upon souls, but they do not want to accept them. You, at least, come to Me as often as possible and take these graces they do not want to accept. In this way you will console My Heart (*Diary*, 367).

Okay, so that's a summary of the Offering to Merciful Love. Now, what's a spiritual communion? It basically consists of making a prayer of desire to receive Jesus in Holy Communion. For instance, one can simply pray: "Lord Jesus, I long to receive you in Holy Communion, but because I can't do so now, I ask you to come into my heart through spiritual communion." Now, if we put the Offering and a spiritual communion together, we get *ecce, fiat, magnificat.* Huh? Something that happened during one of Joe's retreats will teach us what this means.

As Joe was praying and reflecting on the words of the Offering to Merciful Love, he suddenly became aware of his breathing: in/out — in/out — in/out. After a while, he noticed that after he would exhale (out), for a brief moment, before the next inhale (in), his lungs were empty: empty/in/out — empty/in/out — empty/in/out. He reflected on that brief moment of "empty" and began to prolong it by not inhaling right after he exhaled. He would simply hold that moment of "empty lungs" for several seconds before inhaling. Sensing that this breathing exercise was not a distraction from his meditation (the Lord seemed to be leading), he further reflected on the moment of empty. He thought to himself: "This moment of empty is fragile. If I remained in it for long, I'd pass out." He tried to see how long he could hold it. Not long. (Don't worry, he didn't pass out.) He noticed that the inhale sure felt good after holding empty for a while.

Just as Joe began to think this breathing experiment was a waste of time (and a bit silly), three Latin words popped into his mind: *ecce, fiat,* and *magnificat.* Joe understood almost immediately. Each word fit with one of the three moments of breathing. Each word represented a word spoken by Mary in the Bible. Each word following the other was a way of continually making a spiritual communion of merciful love with the Heart of Mary. The Lord answered Joe's request. He not only taught him an easy-to-remember way of continually making a spiritual communion, but he also taught him to do so with Mary. Now I'm going to teach this prayer by explaining two things: first, the three words of Mary and, second, how each of these words corresponds to one of the three moments of breathing.

The Latin word *ecce* means "behold." Mary spoke this word at the Annunciation when the angel Gabriel announced to her that she would be the mother of the Messiah. Mary said, "Behold (*Ecce*), I am the handmaid of the Lord." In other words, she presented herself to the Lord just as she was.

When we pray, God wants us to present ourselves to him as we are, like Mary did. He wants us to say, "*Ecce*," that is, "Behold, here I am, O Lord." Yet there's obviously something very different about Mary and us: We sin; Mary never sinned. Does this fact mean we're unacceptable to the Lord? Absolutely not. Quite the contrary, in fact.

As we learned earlier, we may be tempted to avoid going to Jesus because of our weaknesses, sinfulness, and attachments. But there's no need to be afraid. We console Jesus' Heart when we go to him just as we are — it breaks his Heart when we don't. We don't have to be perfect to go to him. In fact, the weaker and more sinful we are, the more he wants us to go to him and present ourselves with complete honesty and truth, "*Ecce* ... behold, Lord, here I am, sinfulness and all." If only we would always remember how much this pleases him! May we not be afraid to pray, "*Ecce*, here I am, O Lord." May we not give in to the lie that says we're ugly to the Lord.

We are not. We're so beautiful to him just as we are! In fact, his merciful Heart is particularly attracted to the weakest, most sinful souls. My explanation of the next word will say more about this.

The Latin word *fiat* comes from *Fiat mihi*, "Let it be done to me." At the Annunciation, Mary spoke this word after she presented herself to the Lord (*ecce*). Jesus also wants us to speak this word after we present ourselves to him. Yet, when we speak it, it has a bit of a different meaning than Mary's *fiat*. When Mary said, "Let it be done to me," she was allowing the Incarnation of the Word to take place in her immaculate soul. When we say, "Let it be done to me," we're allowing God's merciful love to come pouring down into our weak, sinful souls.

It might be helpful to think of our *fiat* in the following way. First, imagine that the heavens above are an infinite ocean. Next, imagine that this ocean is held back from emptying out onto the earth by a giant floodgate. Well, when we say "*fiat*," it's the magic word that unlocks the gate, and once this gate is unlocked, look out! The waters of the heavenly ocean burst through and pour down into our souls like a great cascading waterfall. But don't be afraid, for as we'll now see, this ocean is a wonderful thing to experience.

As you might have guessed, the ocean I just described is the ocean of God's merciful love. Remember, merciful love is that particular kind of love that seeks out brokenness, suffering, sin, and weakness. Do we understand, then, why Jesus loves it when we go to him as we are, sinfulness and all? It's because weakness and wretchedness is precisely what attracts his merciful love. Thus, he simply (and eagerly) awaits our *fiat*. When we give it, look out! We get washed in the wonderful flood of his merciful love. Now, to the third word spoken by Mary.

The word *magnificat* comes from Mary's exclamation in Latin, *Magnificat anima mea Dominum*, "My soul magnifies the Lord." This is Mary's song of praise when she went to her cousin Elizabeth after giving her *fiat* to the Lord (see Lk 1:46-55). Mary was full of praise because of the "great things" God had done for her. After our fiat, after we've experienced the power of God's merciful love, we, too, will want to give praise to God. We, too, will want to sing out, "*Magnificat!*"

Earlier, I said that the best way to console the Heart of Jesus is by trusting him. I also said that the concrete expression of that trust is praise and thanksgiving. Well, because *magnificat* basically means the same as praise and thanksgiving, when we give our *magnificat* to the Lord, we're consoling him in the best possible way. Of course, sometimes it's easier to praise and thank the Lord than at other times. Moreover, sometimes our praise will have no outward expression at all. It'll just be an act of the will in the depths of our hearts — and that's just fine with Jesus. We give him what we can, and he's happy with that. Nonetheless, when we consider the merciful love that God pours into our hearts, it tends to be much easier to let out an outward song of praise.

Having explained the meaning of the three words, *ecce*, *fiat*, and *magnificat*, now I'm going to apply them to the three moments of our breathing: empty, in, and out.

Recall that Joe thought of "empty" as that brief, fragile moment in between an exhale and an inhale and that he realized if he held it too long, he might pass out. Well, that moment of empty illustrates for us our utter *ecce*. In other words, it shows us what we are of our own sinful selves: empty, weak, and on the verge of passing out. In fact, we can only remain in the moment "empty lungs" for a short time before we pass out and die. This is exactly what we are at ecce. We're saying, "Behold, Lord, here I am — without your mercy, I'll collapse and die." Of course, when we present ourselves to the Lord like this, he rushes to us with his mercy, and we take a deep breath in.

The moment "in" obviously refers to inhale and follows the moment of empty lungs. This moment "in" feels great, especially if we've held empty lungs for 10 to 20 seconds. Go ahead. Try it. Inhale after doing about 20 seconds of empty lungs. Doesn't the inflow of air feel great? Savor it for a moment before you let it go. Hold it for a few moments and enjoy.

What you've just experienced (inhaling) illustrates what happens when we say "*fiat.*" For, when we say it, we allow God's merciful love to flow into our hearts, and it feels great. It's exactly what we need, namely, his mercy entering into our emptiness. Breathe it in.

Now realize this: Each inhale can be a spiritual communion. It becomes one if, when we inhale, we make it our intention to receive God's rejected merciful love into our emptiness. It's especially like receiving Sacramental Communion if we imagine that the merciful love we inhale is coming down from the pierced side of Christ as blood and water. (More on this later.)

Obviously, after we inhale, we'll need to blow the air back out (exhale). This is the "out" moment of breathing. Similarly, after we "inhale" God's merciful love, because it was so good and refreshing, we'll "need" to praise and thank him for the gift of his mercy. This praise and thanks is signified by the air we exhale from our lungs. We give it back to God as an exhaled *magnificat*.

Okay, having explained the meaning of *ecce*, *fiat*, and *magnificat* and having further explained how each of these three words apply to the three moments of our breathing (*ecce*/empty, *fiat*/in, *magnificat*/out), it might be helpful to put it all together with a meditation. For, if we live this breathing exercise as a prayer, then we can constantly be making a spiritual communion, renewing the Offering to Merciful Love, and living praise and thanks. To make our meditation, let's go to the foot of the Cross just before Jesus dies.

Almost everyone else has abandoned him, but Mary is here with you. She puts her words on your lips, "*Ecce* ... Here I am, Lord." You continue: "Here I am, Lord, with all my sinfulness, weaknesses, and attachments. I don't deserve to be here, but I've learned this pleases you. So, behold, O Lord, I come here to console you, even as you are about to die." This humble confidence consoles Jesus right at the moment he breathes his last.

As you pause here in the *ecce* moment with empty lungs, the soldier's lance thrusts through Jesus' side and into his Heart, causing blood and water to flow out and down like a waterfall, down into your heart and soul. As the first drops of this blood and water touch your face, you take a deep breath in, *fiat*. This blood and water (which is his mercy) and this wonderful air (which is also his mercy) fills your soul. After your soul has filled, after your lungs have filled, you linger at the end of the *fiat* moment as you simply enjoy and take delight in his merciful love.

Ah, but after having rested for a brief time in the *fiat* moment, your heart and lungs are ready to release what you've just enjoyed. You're ready to breathe back out to the Lord your love and mercy, your praise and thanks. And so, although he seems to be dead (because this is a meditation, you actually still console him), Mary gently raises you to his lips. You breathe into him your praise and thanks, the love and mercy that his blood and water have given you. In this *magnificat* moment, Jesus' lungs slowly fill with your praise and thanks. Yet his Heart can't hold this returned love, for it's been pierced, and now your lungs are empty. Don't worry. Mary gently lowers you to the foot of the Cross where the blood and water again begin to flow down from the Lord's pierced side and into your emptiness, into the poverty of your ecce. And so begins again that wonderful cycle of love and mercy: *ecce*/empty — *fiat*/in — *magnificat*/out — *ecce*/empty — *fiat*/in — *magnificat*/out.

If we live this attitude of presenting our wretchedness to the Lord (*ecce*), receiving his mercy (*fiat*), and then praising and thanking him for his saving mercy (*magnificat*), we can be assured that we won't seriously be wounding the Lord by our lack of trust — for trust is not only praise and thanks, it's also to receive God's mercy. Remember how I said that to live trust means to praise and thank God for everything? Some people might have read that and thought, "Hmmm. That's all well and good, but I don't always feel full of praise and thanks, especially when it's hard to be grateful because of life's hurts." Isn't that the truth? But look at what we've just learned from the *ecce, fiat, magnificat* movement: The path to praise begins with the *ecce* moment. Moreover, while we're in the ecce moment, we normally don't feel like praising and thanking, and that's all right. For, from the *ecce* moment, we eventually move to the fiat moment, that is, we call down (*fiat*) the Lord's blood and water (*mercy*) into our emptiness. Then, that *fiat* moment eventually leads to *magnificat*, to praise and thanks.

Don't worry if you're in the ecce moment for a long time. For the simple act of presenting yourself to the Lord as you are, sinfulness and all, is itself an act of trust. Furthermore, the act of receiving God's merciful love (*fiat*) is also an act of trust, and both these acts of trust (*ecce* and *fiat*) tend to lead to a further act of trust, namely, praise and thanks (*magnificat*).

5. THE INSENSITIVITY OF OUR HEARTS

Hardness of heart is the opposite of mercy. It separates us from God, is the loss of our humanity, and causes so much suffering. To one degree or another, all of us have hardened hearts that need healing. Such is the sad effect of sin in our lives.

Up to this point, everything we've covered in this prayer companion has been about healing our hearts. In other words, it's been about making our hearts more compassionate to the suffering of the Sacred Heart of Jesus. Now, while our focus still involves healing for our hardened hearts, we're going to try something new: We're going to hone in on feeling compassion for the suffering of our neighbor. We're going to focus not so much on growing in compassion for the suffering of Jesus, the Head of the Mystical Body, but on growing in compassion for the suffering of the members of his Mystical Body.

Because mercy is a twofold movement of compassion and action, this section is divided into two main sections. The first section deals with becoming more compassionate to the suffering of our neighbor. The second section deals with the action needed to alleviate that suffering.

(a) Becoming Sensitive to the Suffering of Our Neighbor

Meditate on the Passion of Christ

The best way to grow in compassion for the suffering of our neighbor is to meditate on the Passion of Christ. Well, that's actually what our principle and foundation is all about, namely, keeping the sorrow and suffering of Christ always before the eyes of our souls.

The Diary of St. Faustina gives testimony to the power of meditating on the Passion for healing our hearts. Jesus tells Faustina, **"My daughter, your compassion for Me refreshes Me. By meditating on My Passion, your soul acquires a distinct beauty"** (1657). Notice two things here. First, Jesus is consoled ("refreshed") by Faustina's compassion. Second, Faustina is changed. That is, her soul "acquires a distinct beauty." What beauty? I suggest it's the beauty of a soul (heart) that's growing in compassion. And what's the means to such growth? According to Jesus, it's meditation on his Passion.

Meditating on the Passion of Jesus contains yet another gift. While the suffering of others evokes our compassion and thus helps heal our hearts, the suffering of Jesus carries with it an extraordinary gift of grace. When we prayerfully reflect on the Passion, God's grace powerfully works in our hearts to help us experience compassion and healing — but don't just take my word for it. After lamenting that few souls reflect on his Passion with true feeling, Jesus said to St. Faustina, **"I give great graces to souls who meditate devoutly on My Passion"** (*Diary*, 737).

Examination of Conscience

All sin hardens our hearts, but some sins are particularly effective in doing so. Let's take a brief look at some specific kinds of sin that do the best job of hardening our hearts, and let's begin with a prayer to the Holy Spirit.

PRAYER. Come, Holy Spirit. Come, you who can open my eyes to the reality of sin. Help me to see the areas in my life that harden my heart and make it insensitive to the suffering of my neighbor. Holy Spirit, speak to me during this examination of conscience. Show me what's wounding my heart. Help me to overcome sin in my life that I may ponder Christ's Passion with true feeling, that my heart may be renewed, and that I may respond to my neighbor's suffering with deeper compassion and more generous mercy.

GOSSIP AND ENVY. Gossip and envy are especially effective at hardening hearts because of the way they twist our emotional responses to the suffering of others. So, for example, instead of feeling sorry for someone who suffers, gossip and envy get us to rejoice and delight over his suffering. In the case of gossip, this kind of emotional perversion may not happen immediately, but it leads in this direction. Envy is more directly destructive. By its very nature, it leads to a kind of wicked celebration over the misfortune of others whose goods we want for ourselves.

Regarding gossip: Do I have a morbid curiosity? For instance, when I watch the news, do I become interested in catastrophes, murders, or atrocities of war as a kind of entertainment? Or, when I hear of such sad situations, do I immediately pray for the people affected? Do I take delight in hearing of scandals? If I begin to feel an intense interest in some scandal, am I quick to mortify my curiosity? Do I engage in the kind of gossip that repeats the sins or misfortunes of others for no good reason? (detraction). Or worse, do I harm the reputation of others by speaking falsely about them? (calumny). Do I take too much interest in rumors and the doings of others? Do I choose as my friends people who like to gossip about others? Do I watch television shows, visit websites, or read magazines that tend toward gossip? Do I give some thought to what I say about others? Do I speak too much about others? Do I do some critical reflection after a conversation about others that has left me feeling uneasy?

Regarding envy: Do I become sad when I see the material or spiritual wealth of others? Do I rejoice or take delight in the misfortunes or falls of someone whom I envy? If I experience such emotions in myself, do I act against them by praying for the person and turning my thoughts to something else? Or do I linger with the perverted delight and nurture it by continually reflecting on the "good news" of someone else's misfortune? Do I take what I have for granted? Or am I aware of and thankful for what God has given to me and my family?

LUST AND GREED. Sins that habituate us to seeing our neighbor as an object (instead of as a person) are particularly good at making us blind to the suffering of others. Such sins include lust, whereby we see others simply as objects for sexual pleasure, and greed, whereby we see others merely as opportunities for (or obstacles to) making money.

Regarding lust: Do I tend to see others as sexual objects? Do I look at pornography? Do I keep a healthy custody of my eyes, especially during spring and summer months when people often dress immodestly? If I catch my eyes turning to where they shouldn't go, do I give the "second look" to God? Or do I allow my eyes to continue their pursuit? If I'm tempted with impure thoughts, do I turn to prayer? Or do I linger with them and their sinful delight? Do I avoid the near occasion of sin by avoiding forms of entertainment and places that might especially tempt me to impurity? Do I avoid idleness? Or do I waste time and give in to laziness? (Being idle and lazy invites temptations to impurity.)

Regarding greed: Do I see people only as potential clients and miss seeing them as persons? Are things more important to me than people? Am I driven to seek ways of making excessive amounts of money? If I'm married, am I open to life? Or do I have a contraceptive mentality, valuing a fancy car or exotic vacations more than having another child? Do I distinguish needs from wants? Have I always got to have the latest thing or a name brand? Can I enjoy the simple pleasures of life? Am I generous in giving to the poor?

JUDGMENTAL ATTITUDE. As Blessed Mother Teresa used to say, "If you take the time to judge, you don't have time to love." When we assume an attitude of judgment toward another, a gap yawns between us and them, and we can't connect. This is a diabolical attitude that stems from pride. It's subtle, but it does more damage to the heart than sins of the flesh — the very same sins over which it often sits in judgment.

Do I see myself as superior to others? Do I look down on particular groups of people because of their race, opinions, or ways of life? Do I impute motives to the actions of others, or do I leave such judgments to God? Am I quick to judge priests and bishops, or do I leave them, especially, to God's judgment? Do I pray for priests and bishops? Do I tend to make rash judgments of others? In other words, do I assume as true, without sufficient foundation, the moral faults of others? Do I realize rash judgment is grave matter when it rashly judges acts that are grave? To avoid rash judgment, am I careful, as the *Catechism* says, "to interpret insofar as possible [my] neighbor's thoughts, words, and deeds in a favorable way"? (2478). Am I insecure in my own life of faith and judge others out of a need to feel righteous? Or, while striving for holiness, do I recognize my own weaknesses, sinfulness, and attachments and go to Jesus, whom I know is rich in mercy? Do I relate to the older brother in the parable of the Prodigal Son? (see Lk 15:11-32). Do I believe in God's mercy? Do I realize that those who are merciful will obtain mercy (see Mt 5:7) and that the measure I give will be the measure I get back? (see Lk 6:38).

UNWILLINGNESS TO FORGIVE. Here I've saved what may be the "worst" for last. Nothing hardens a heart more than an unwillingness to forgive. When we cling to bitterness, resentment, grudges, and hate for those who have hurt us, our hearts quickly become as cold and hard as ice. When we don't forgive, we may think we're punishing the other person, but the reality is we're destroying ourselves. We often pray to our heavenly Father, "Forgive us our trespasses as we forgive those who trespass against us." Do we realize that if we don't forgive, we won't be forgiven? Still, we need not get discouraged or despair if we struggle in this area, for if we have even the slightest bit of good will, the Lord's mercy is there for us. Moreover, he knows that it often takes time for us to be able to forgive fully, and he's patient. O Lord, please give us the grace to forgive!

Are there people in my life whom I haven't forgiven? Do I hold on to bitterness over past wounds? Am I resentful toward anyone? Is there anyone to whom I give the silent treatment? Is there anyone I would refuse to help if he needed it? Do I pray for my enemies? Is there anyone for whom I would not pray? Do I need to ask anyone for forgiveness?

Is there anyone with whom it might be helpful to talk regarding a past hurt that especially bothers me, and can I do so without being accusatory and with a readiness to forgive? Have I asked Jesus for the grace to forgive? Do I reflect on how often Jesus has forgiven me? Do I reflect on his example of forgiving those who crucified him? Do I realize my sins crucified him? Do I realize he still loves me when I choose to forgive but struggle with forgetting? Do I try to forget? Or do I continually replay in my mind past hurts? Do I try to give people a clean slate? Have I said, "I forgive you"? Do I try to forgive? Or do I give in to anger, which seeks to do evil to someone out of a desire for revenge? According to St. Faustina, "We resemble God most when we forgive our neighbors" (*Diary*, 1148).

Okay, that examination of conscience might have been a bit heavy. If you want to go to confession soon, then by all means, go for it. (Before going, I suggest you read the section "Confession" in Appendix Two of *Consoling the Heart of Jesus,* henceforth "*CHJ.*")

Confession is great, but getting down on oneself is not. If the spiritual exercise we just read has got you beating yourself up, please stop. Yes, stop beating yourself and, instead, start reflecting on what we learned in the Second Obstacle about our weaknesses, sinfulness, and attachments. Also, before you start reading the next section, you might want to spend some time with the Lord — actually, that's a good idea for all of us. Even if we didn't start getting down on ourselves, let's all spend some time going to Jesus as we are with all our weaknesses, sinfulness, and attachments (*ecce*). Then, let's console Jesus (and ourselves) by allowing his merciful love to wash over us (*fiat*). Finally, after having spent some time praising him for his superabundant mercy (*magnificat*), let's get back to the *Prayer Companion*. See you in a little while.

(b) Having Mercy on Our Neighbor in Deed, Word, and Prayer

Jesus once gave St. Faustina an amazingly simple yet profound lesson on having mercy on others. She records it in her *Diary*:

> **I am giving you three ways of exercising mercy toward your neighbor: the first — by deed, the second — by word, the third — by prayer. In these three degrees is contained the fullness of mercy, and it is an unquestionable proof of love for Me. By this means a soul glorifies and pays reverence to My mercy** (742).

Faustina deepens this lesson for us by elaborating on the "three degrees" of mercy in the following passage:

> The first: the act of mercy, of whatever kind. The second: the word of mercy — if I cannot carry out a work of mercy, I will assist by my words. The third: prayer — if I cannot show mercy by deeds or words, I can always do so by prayer. My prayer reaches out even there where I cannot reach out physically (163).

Now, let's look more closely at each of these three degrees, beginning with the first degree: deeds of mercy.

Deed: The Merciful Outlook

There are infinite ways of doing deeds of mercy. To give some organization to them, theologians have divided the "works of mercy" into two categories: spiritual and corporal. Each category, they say, contains seven works of mercy, making for a grand total of 14. Yet reflecting on 14 points is still a lot, especially if we've only got a short time for this reflection. (Those who want to reflect on them after using the *Prayer Companion* can find them in "References and Notes" in *CHJ*.) So, instead of fourteen points, I'd like to present just one simple and effective way of practicing deeds of mercy. I call it the "merciful outlook." I like this way a lot because it's a deed of mercy we can practice almost anytime (provided we're around other people).

What is the merciful outlook? It's a subtle way of seeing others that communicates to them a simple and sincere message, "I delight that you exist." This felt delight in others, expressed in the merciful outlook, stems from grasping the truth and beauty of who the other authentically is. And who is the other? The other is Christ. The other is Christ insofar as he's a member of Christ's Mystical Body (or, if he's not a Christian, he's a prospective member of Christ by virtue of his being made in the image of God and called to full membership in Christ's Body). In a mystical yet very real way, the other truly is Christ.

Moreover, the merciful outlook is …

- truly merciful, because it recognizes that mercy is a bilateral reality such that as we give we also receive — thus, it isn't a patronizing outlook;

- evangelization, proclaiming the good news of Christ's love through an authentic love for the other person — thus, it's not a proselytizing outlook;

- a response to existential loneliness that gives a cup of love to help quench our neighbor's thirst as well as our own;

- the gaze of God: It sees the good in others and brings it to light, draws it out — thus, it's not a judgmental outlook, which focuses on and draws out evil;

- wonderful, because of the sense of awe and wonder we feel at seeing the other as an unrepeatable manifestation of Christ's own beauty;

- a loving gaze that says, "You are great," because it sees the true greatness as well as the potential for greatness in the other;

- deep-sea diving: knowing there is buried treasure in the other, a facet of the face of Christ not found in any other, and swimming through murky waters to find it;

- something that takes courage and perseverance because it sometimes meets with misunderstanding, coldness, and rejection;

- to truly delight in each and every person we meet, because we see in each one the unique member of the Body of Christ he is;

- loving others with the Heart of Christ, because each of us is a member of his body and thus shares the same Heart with him.

Word: The Merciful Question

A merciful word is anything written or said with the intention of alleviating the suffering of another. For example, a word that aims to give hope to the despairing, tries to get the sad to laugh, attempts to help the fearful to trust in Jesus, or seeks to make the lonely feel less alone is a word of mercy. Here, I'd like to focus on one specific word of mercy. It's actually a question. I call it the "merciful question."

The merciful question goes with the merciful outlook. Recall that the merciful outlook responds to the suffering of another's thirst for love by expressing delight in him. Well, the merciful question is simply a way of helping us to experience this delight in the other. It does so by inviting the other (by means of a question) to open up, reveal his treasure, and show who he is.

We ourselves should be open to answering the merciful questions others pose to us. As Pope John Paul II wrote in his encyclical letter *Dives in Misericordia*, mercy is a "bilateral reality" (14). Thus, while the one who shares receives the gift of being listened to, there's also a gift for the person who gets to listen, who gets to see the treasure of the other open up. We all have inner riches, and we shouldn't be afraid to share them with others. However, we might want to make sure that the other really is open (maybe their question was just small talk), and we might want to strive not to flood them with words.

Prayer: The Chaplet of Divine Mercy and Modified "Breathing Prayer"

According to St. Faustina, if we can't do a deed of mercy or speak a word of mercy, we can always reach out to others spiritually through our prayers. How do we do this, specifically? From among the infinite ways of offering prayers of mercy, I'd like to make two recommendations: the Chaplet of Divine Mercy and a modified "breathing prayer."

CHAPLET OF DIVINE MERCY. In the context of the First Obstacle of the *Consoling the Heart of Jesus* retreat, I spoke about the power of the Chaplet of Divine Mercy. (See *CHJ*, page 72.) Because it's so mighty, I suggest we adopt it as one of our prayers of mercy. Building on what I said earlier, I'd like to explain further why the chaplet is so awesome.

The chaplet is particularly effective as a prayer, because through it we offer the suffering of Jesus to the Father. In fact, because of this action, the chaplet is the most powerful prayer there is. On hearing this, perhaps someone might say, "Wait a minute. I thought the Mass was the most efficacious prayer." That's right. It is — and that's the whole point. The chaplet is a kind of extension of the prayer of the Mass. For, in the chaplet, as in the Mass (and in union with the Mass), we offer the Body and Blood of Christ to the Father — along with our own joys, sorrows, sufferings, and prayers. Because of this connection between the chaplet and the Mass, I recommend that whenever we pray the chaplet, we consciously unite our praying of it to the prayer of all the Masses being said throughout the world.

To help us appreciate better the power of the chaplet, I'd now like to present a few selections from the *Diary of St. Faustina*. The first selection provides an instance of how the chaplet can help those who face material evils. Faustina writes:

> Today I was awakened by a great storm. The wind was raging, and it was raining in torrents, thunderbolts striking again and again. I began to pray that the storm would do no harm, when I heard the words: **Say the chaplet I have taught you, and**

the storm will cease. I began immediately to say the chaplet and hadn't even finished it when the storm suddenly ceased, and I heard the words: **Through the chaplet you will obtain everything, if what you ask for is compatible with My will** (1731).

The second selection has to do with the power of the chaplet to help those in spiritual need. In the following, St. Faustina describes what happened after Jesus asked her to help him save a certain despairing soul by praying the chaplet for him:

> Suddenly, I found myself in a strange cottage where an elderly man was dying amidst great torments. All about the bed was a multitude of demons and the family, who were crying. When I began to pray [the chaplet], the spirits of darkness fled, with hissing and threats directed at me. The soul became calm and, filled with trust, rested in the Lord.
>
> At the same moment, I found myself again in my own room. How this happens ... I do not know (1797-1798).

In relating events like this, St. Faustina was simply following the instructions of the

Lord, who had said to her: "**My daughter, encourage souls to say the chaplet which I have given to you. It pleases Me to grant everything they ask of Me by saying the chaplet**" (1541). May St. Faustina's testimony to the power of the chaplet encourage us to pray it with greater fervor and bolder confidence. (To read more of her testimony on the power of the chaplet, see the section "Chaplet of Divine Mercy" in Appendix Two of *CHJ*.)

Okay, so we realize the Chaplet of Divine Mercy is a powerful prayer. Yet, as we begin to pray it, some of us might wonder, "Well, for whom should I pray?" Of course, prayers of mercy are for anyone who's in need of mercy … but that's everyone! Moreover, maybe you're one of those people who, like me, finds it difficult to pray for general things (like "the whole world"). For those of us who run into such problems with intercessory prayer, I have two bits of advice.

First, give the rights to the grace (merit) of your prayers to Mary (which, by the way, is part of what it means to be consecrated to her). In other words, tell her, "Mary, I give you the right to distribute the grace of my prayers as you see fit." Making such a gift to her has a big benefit. It ensures that the grace of our prayers will be used in the best way possible, and thus it can relieve our anxiety about who to pray for.

It works like this: Because of her unique vantage point from heaven, and on account of her most intimate communion with her Divine Son, Mary can best determine which people are most in need of our prayers. For instance, seeing some forgotten person in China about to die in despair, Mary can take the grace of our prayers (and "offered up" sufferings) and use it to help that dying person to trust in God and accept salvation.

Now, perhaps this idea has got some of us thinking:

> Well, that's great. I'm happy to help the dying person in China, whom I don't know, but I'd be disappointed if I therefore couldn't use the grace of my prayers to help the people I do know, like my family and friends. I'm worried that if I give Mary "first rights," then I'll lose the right to pray for those whom I especially love, even if they're less in need than other people in the world.

This is a legitimate concern, but there's no need to worry. Remember how we read earlier that Mary makes the good things we give to her more perfect? (see pages 53-54). Well, it's true. She increases the grace of such good things as our prayers, and she works to make sure there's enough to go around. Moreover, we should keep in mind that Mary is not out-done in generosity. If we're so generous as to give her the right to distribute the grace of our prayers, she'll surely be especially generous to our loved ones. In fact, she'll take even better care of our loved ones than we ourselves can. For instance, let's say one of our family members or friends is in need of prayer, and we don't know it. Well, Mary knows it, and she'll make sure that that person doesn't go without.

Giving Mary the right to distribute the grace of our prayers doesn't mean we can't still pray for our loved ones. We can and should pray for them. It's just that we reserve to Mary the "first right," so to speak, to distribute the grace of our prayers. Now then, if we can and should still pray for others, the question remains, "For whom should I pray the Chaplet of Divine Mercy?" This brings us to my second bit of advice: If you're looking for specific mercy intentions, you might want to begin to pray a continuous Novena to Divine Mercy. Allow me to explain.

In the Novena to Divine Mercy, Jesus asked St. Faustina to pray for nine different groups of people. (See "Novena to Divine Mercy" in Part Three of the *Prayer Companion*.) To pray a continuous Novena to Divine Mercy simply means praying for one of those nine groups of people each day while reciting the chaplet, and then, after nine days, starting over. I find this a helpful way to focus my prayer. Along with or instead of this, I suggest praying for the people who are most in need of mercy, namely, unrepentant sinners, especially for those who are dying. Jesus told Faustina that prayer for sinners is the most pleasing to him and that nobody is more in need of trust than the dying. As we learned from the story about the man dying in the cottage, great battles are waged for despairing souls at the hour of death. Let's help Jesus save them by praying the chaplet.

MODIFIED "BREATHING PRAYER." Having spent some time reflecting on the Chaplet of Divine Mercy as a way of showing mercy through prayer, we're now ready to turn our attention to my next suggestion for doing prayers of mercy. Like the chaplet, the prayer I'm now going to suggest is based on a prayer that Jesus taught St. Faustina. Also, it includes the "breathing prayer" we learned earlier. In order to explain it, I'm going to start with the prayer that Jesus taught Faustina. He said to her:

> **Call upon My mercy on behalf of sinners; I desire their salvation. When you say this prayer, with a contrite heart and with faith on behalf of some sinner, I will give**

him the grace of conversion. This is the prayer: "O Blood and Water, which gushed forth from the Heart of Jesus as a fount of mercy for us, I trust in You" (*Diary*, 186).

Did you catch the Lord's promise? He said, **"When you say this prayer, with a contrite heart and with faith on behalf of some sinner,** *I will give him the grace of conversion.***"** That's quite a promise. Because this "O Blood and Water" prayer is so powerful, I suggest we make a deal with the Lord by praying the following:

Lord, you can understand people in any language, including sign language. Well, I'd like to translate the "O Blood and Water" prayer into sign language. So, Lord, I propose the following deal. Anytime I consciously inhale with the intention of receiving the blood and water that gushed forth from your pierced side [recall the *fiat* moment of the breathing prayer, which implies contrition], I ask you to fill me with your merciful love. Then, when I exhale with the intention of giving this mercy to others, I ask you to give them the grace of the "O

Blood and Water" prayer, namely, the grace of conversion.

Does this deal seem too bold? When it comes to asking for graces for sinners, nothing is too bold for the soul that trusts in God's mercy. In fact, we can read example after example from the lives of saints such as Faustina and Thérèse of mind-blowing boldness in prayer. The Lord accepted their bold petitions, because he was so pleased with the trust in his mercy that inspired them. To Faustina, he even emphasized that anything she might say to express the generosity of his mercy would always fall well short of the reality (*Diary*, 1273, 1605). Moreover, he also emphasized that the more a soul trusts in his mercy the more it will receive (1578).

Okay, so it's not too bold to make the sign-language prayer deal with Jesus. Therefore, let's make the deal and begin exhaling God's mercy. The best part about the prayer is that it isn't complicated. It's as straightforward as breathing. We can simply walk down the street and pray for everyone we pass, trustfully exhaling superabundant mercy on them. Still, simple doesn't mean easy. Such intercession does take concentration and a spirit of prayer.

PART THREE

Prayers and
Plan of Life

A. PRAYERS

1. DIVINE MERCY PRAYERS

Chaplet of Divine Mercy
(*Diary*, 475-476)

The Chaplet of Divine Mercy is recited using ordinary rosary beads of five decades. The Chaplet is preceded by two opening prayers from the Diary of Saint Faustina *(1319, 84), followed by a closing prayer (446), and a second, optional, closing prayer (950).*

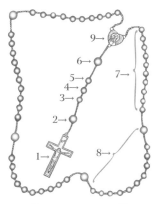

(1) MAKE THE SIGN OF THE CROSS

In the name of the Father, and of the Son, and of the Holy Spirit. Amen.

(2) OPTIONAL OPENING PRAYERS

You expired, Jesus, but the source of life gushed forth for souls, and the ocean of mercy opened up for the whole world. O Fount of Life, unfathomable Divine Mercy, envelop the whole world and empty Yourself out upon us. ... O Blood and Water, which gushed forth from the Heart of Jesus as a fountain of Mercy for us, I trust in You!

(3) OUR FATHER

Our Father, who art in heaven, hallowed be Thy name; Thy kingdom come; Thy will be done on earth as it is in heaven. Give us this day our daily bread; and forgive us our trespasses as we forgive those who trespass against us; and lead us not into temptation, but deliver us from evil. Amen.

(4) HAIL MARY

Hail Mary, full of grace. The Lord is with thee. Blessed art thou amongst women, and blessed is the fruit of thy womb, Jesus. Holy Mary, Mother of God, pray for us sinners, now and at the hour of our death. Amen.

(5) THE APOSTLE'S CREED

I believe in God, the Father almighty, Creator of heaven and earth, and in Jesus Christ, his only Son, our Lord, who was conceived by the Holy Spirit, born of the

Virgin Mary, suffered under Pontius Pilate, was crucified, died, and was buried; he descended into hell; on the third day he rose again from the dead; he ascended into heaven, and is seated at the right hand of God the Father almighty; from there he will come to judge the living and the dead. I believe in the Holy Spirit, the holy catholic Church, the communion of saints, the forgiveness of sins, the resurrection of the body, and life everlasting. Amen.

(6) THE ETERNAL FATHER

Eternal Father, I offer you the Body and Blood, Soul and Divinity of Your Dearly Beloved Son, Our Lord, Jesus Christ, in atonement for our sins and those of the whole world.

(7) ON THE TEN SMALL BEADS OF EACH DECADE

For the sake of His sorrowful Passion, have mercy on us and on the whole world.

(8) REPEAT FOR THE REMAINING DECADES

Saying the "Eternal Father" (6) on the "Our Father" bead and then "For the sake of His sorrowful Passion" (7) on the following "Hail Mary" beads.

(9) Conclude with Holy God
(Repeat Three Times)

Holy God, Holy Mighty One, Holy Immortal One, have mercy on us and on the whole world.

(10) Optional Closing Prayer

Eternal God, in whom mercy is endless and the treasury of compassion — inexhaustible, look kindly upon us and increase Your mercy in us, that in difficult moments we might not despair nor become despondent, but with great confidence submit ourselves to Your holy will, which is Love and Mercy itself.

The Divine Mercy Novena
(*Diary*, 1209-1229)

First Day:

Today bring to Me ALL MANKIND, ESPECIALLY ALL SINNERS, and immerse them in the ocean of My mercy. In this way you will console Me in the bitter grief into which the loss of souls plunges Me.

Most Merciful Jesus, whose very nature it is to have compassion on us and to forgive us, do not look upon our sins but upon our trust which we place in Your infinite goodness. Receive us all into the abode of Your Most

Compassionate Heart, and never let us escape from It. We beg this of You by Your love which unites You to the Father and the Holy Spirit.

Eternal Father, turn Your merciful gaze upon all mankind and especially upon poor sinners, all enfolded in the Most Compassionate Heart of Jesus. For the sake of His sorrowful Passion, show us Your mercy, that we may praise the omnipotence of Your mercy forever and ever. Amen.

SECOND DAY:

Today bring to Me THE SOULS OF PRIESTS AND RELIGIOUS, and immerse them in My unfathomable mercy. It was they who gave Me strength to endure My bitter Passion. Through them as through channels My mercy flows out upon mankind.

Most Merciful Jesus, from whom comes all that is good, increase Your grace in men and women consecrated to Your service,* that they may perform worthy works of mercy; and that all who see them may glorify the Father of Mercy who is in heaven.

Eternal Father, turn Your merciful gaze upon the company of chosen ones in Your vineyard—upon the souls of priests and religious; and endow them with the strength of Your blessing. For the love of the Heart of Your Son in which they are enfolded, impart to them Your power and light, that they may be able to guide others in the way of salvation and with one voice sing praise to Your boundless mercy for ages without end. Amen.

*In the original text, St. Faustina uses the pronoun "us" since she was offering this prayer as a consecrated religious sister. The wording adapted here is intended to make the prayer suitable for universal use.

THIRD DAY:

Today bring to Me ALL DEVOUT AND FAITHFUL SOULS, and immerse them in the ocean of My mercy. In this way you will console Me in the bitter grief into which the loss of souls plunges Me.

Most Merciful Jesus, from the treasury of Your mercy, You impart Your graces in great abundance to each and all. Receive us into the abode of Your Most Compassionate Heart and never let us escape from It. We beg this grace of You by that most wonderous love for the heavenly Father with which Your Heart burns so fiercely.

Eternal Father, turn Your merciful gaze upon faithful souls, as upon the inheritance of Your Son. For the sake of His sorrowful Passion, grant them Your blessing and surround them with Your constant protection. Thus may they never fail in love or lose the treasure of the holy faith, but rather, with all the hosts of Angels and Saints, may they glorify Your boundless mercy for endless ages. Amen.

FOURTH DAY:

Today bring to Me THOSE WHO DO NOT BELIEVE IN GOD* AND THOSE WHO DO NOT YET KNOW ME. I was thinking also of them during My bitter Passion, and their future zeal comforted My Heart. Immerse them in the ocean of My mercy.

Most compassionate Jesus, You are the Light of the whole world. Receive into the abode of Your Most Compassionate Heart the souls of those who do not believe in God and of those who as yet do not know You. Let the rays of Your grace enlighten them that they, too, together with us, may extol Your wonderful mercy; and do not let them escape from the abode which is Your Most Compassionate Heart.

Eternal Father, turn Your merciful gaze upon the souls of those who do not believe in You, and of those who as yet do not know You, but who are enclosed in the Most Compassionate Heart of Jesus. Draw them to the light of the Gospel. These souls do not know what great happiness it is to love You. Grant that they, too, may extol the generosity of Your mercy for endless ages. Amen.

*Our Lord's original words here were "the pagans." Since the pontificate of Pope John XXIII, the Church has seen fit to replace this term with clearer and more appropriate terminology.

FIFTH DAY:

Today bring to Me THE SOULS OF THOSE WHO HAVE SEPARATED THEMSELVES FROM MY CHURCH,* and immerse them in the ocean of My mercy. During My bitter Passion they tore at My Body and Heart, that is, My Church. As they return to unity with the Church, My wounds heal and in this way they alleviate My Passion.

Most Merciful Jesus, Goodness Itself, You do not refuse light to those who seek it of You. Receive into the abode of Your Most Compassionate Heart the souls of those who have separated themselves from Your Church. Draw them by Your light into the unity of the Church, and do not let them escape from the abode of Your Most Compassionate Heart; but bring it about that they, too, come to glorify the generosity of Your mercy.

Eternal Father, turn Your merciful gaze upon the souls of those who have separated themselves from Your Son's Church, who have squandered Your blessings and misused Your graces by obstinately persisting in their errors. Do not look upon their errors, but upon the love of Your own Son and upon His bitter Passion, which He underwent for their sake, since they, too, are enclosed in His Most Compassionate Heart. Bring it about that they also may glorify Your great mercy for endless ages. Amen.

*Our Lord's original words here were "heretics and schismatics," since He spoke to Saint Faustina within the context of her times. As of the Second Vatican Council, Church authorities have seen fit not to use those designations in accordance with the explanation given in the Council's Decree on Ecumenism (n.3). Every pope since the Council has reaffirmed that usage. Saint Faustina herself, her heart always in harmony with the mind of the Church, most certainly would have agreed. When at one time, because of the decisions of her superiors and Father confessor, she was not able to execute Our Lord's inspirations and orders, she declared: "I will follow Your will insofar as You will permit me to do so through Your representative. O my Jesus, I give priority to the voice of the Church over the voice with which You speak to me" (Diary, 497). The Lord confirmed her action and praised her for it.

Sixth Day:

Today bring to Me **THE MEEK AND HUMBLE SOULS AND THE SOULS OF LITTLE CHILDREN,** and immerse them in My mercy. These souls most closely resemble My Heart. They strengthened Me during My bitter agony. I saw them as earthly Angels, who will keep vigil at My altars. I pour out upon them whole torrents of grace. Only the humble soul is capable of receiving My grace. I favor humble souls with My confidence.

Most Merciful Jesus, You Yourself have said, "Learn from Me for I am meek and humble of heart." Receive into the abode of Your Most Compassionate Heart all meek and humble souls and the souls of little children. These souls send all heaven into ecstasy and they are the heavenly Father's favorites. They are a sweet-smelling bouquet before the throne of God; God Himself takes delight in their fragrance. These souls have a permanent abode in Your Most Compassionate Heart, O Jesus, and they unceasingly sing out a hymn of love and mercy.

Eternal Father, turn Your merciful gaze upon meek souls, upon humble souls, and upon little children who are enfolded in the abode which is the Most Compassionate Heart of Jesus. These souls bear the closest resemblance to Your Son. Their fragrance rises from the earth and reaches Your very throne. Father of mercy and of all goodness, I beg You by the love You bear these souls and by the delight You take in them: Bless the whole world, that all souls together may sing out the praises of Your mercy for endless ages. Amen.

SEVENTH DAY:

Today bring to Me **THE SOULS WHO ESPECIALLY VENERATE AND GLORIFY MY MERCY,*** and immerse them in My mercy. These souls sorrowed

most over my Passion and entered most deeply into My spirit. They are living images of My Compassionate Heart. These souls will shine with a special brightness in the next life. Not one of them will go into the fire of hell. I shall particularly defend each one of them at the hour of death.

Most Merciful Jesus, whose Heart is Love Itself, receive into the abode of Your Most Compassionate Heart the souls of those who particularly extol and venerate the greatness of Your mercy. These souls are mighty with the very power of God Himself. In the midst of all afflictions and adversities they go forward, confident of Your mercy; and united to You, O Jesus, they carry all mankind on their shoulders. These souls will not be judged severely, but Your mercy will embrace them as they depart from this life.

Eternal Father, turn Your merciful gaze upon the souls who glorify and venerate Your greatest attribute, that of Your fathomless mercy, and who are enclosed in the Most Compassionate Heart of Jesus. These souls are a living Gospel; their hands are full of deeds of mercy, and their hearts, overflowing with joy, sing a canticle of mercy to You, O Most High! I beg You O God:

Show them Your mercy according to
the hope and trust they have placed

in You. Let there be accomplished in them the promise of Jesus, who said to them that during their life, but especially at the hour of death, the souls who will venerate this fathomless mercy of His, He, Himself, will defend as His glory. Amen.

*The text leads one to conclude that in the first prayer directed to Jesus, who is the Redeemer, it is "victim" souls and contemplatives that are being prayed for; those persons, that is, that voluntarily offered themselves to God for the salvation of their neighbor (see Col 1:24; 2 Cor 4:12). This explains their close union with the Savior and the extraordinary efficacy that their invisible activity has for others. In the second prayer, directed to the Father from whom comes "every worthwhile gift and every genuine benefit," we recommend the "active" souls, who promote devotion to The Divine Mercy and exercise with it all the other works that lend themselves to the spiritual and material uplifting of their brethren.

EIGHTH DAY:

Today bring to Me **THE SOULS WHO ARE DETAINED IN PURGATORY**, and immerse them in the abyss of My mercy. Let the torrents of My Blood cool down their scorching flames. All these souls are greatly loved by Me. They are making retribution to My justice. It is in your power to bring them relief. Draw all the indulgences from the treasury of My Church and offer them on their behalf. **Oh, if you only knew the torments they suffer, you would continually offer for them the alms of the spirit and pay off their debt to My justice.**

Most Merciful Jesus, You Yourself have said that You desire mercy; so I bring into the abode of Your Most Compassionate Heart the souls in Purgatory, souls who are very dear to You, and yet, who must make retribution to Your justice. May the streams of Blood and Water which gushed forth from Your Heart put out the flames of Purgatory, that there, too, the power of Your mercy may be celebrated.

Eternal Father, turn Your merciful gaze upon the souls suffering in Purgatory, who are enfolded in the Most Compassionate Heart of Jesus. I beg You, by the sorrowful Passion of Jesus Your Son, and by all the bitterness with which His most sacred Soul was flooded: Manifest Your mercy to the souls who are under Your just scrutiny. Look upon them in no other way but only through the Wounds of Jesus, Your dearly beloved Son; for we firmly believe that there is no limit to Your goodness and compassion. Amen.

NINTH DAY:

Today bring to Me SOULS WHO HAVE BECOME LUKEWARM,* and immerse them in the abyss of My mercy.

These souls wound My Heart most painfully. My soul suffered the most dreadful loathing in the Garden of Olives because of luke-warm souls. They were the reason I cried out: "Father, take this cup away from Me, if it be Your will." For them, the last hope of salvation is to run to My mercy.

Most compassionate Jesus, You are Compassion Itself. I bring lukewarm souls into the abode of Your Most Compassionate Heart. In this fire of Your pure love, let these tepid souls, who, like corpses, filled You with such deep loathing, be once again set aflame. O Most Compassionate Jesus, exercise the omnipotence of Your mercy and draw them into the very ardor of Your love, and bestow upon them the gift of holy love, for nothing is beyond Your power.

Eternal Father, turn Your merciful gaze upon lukewarm souls who are nonetheless enfolded in the Most Compassionate Heart of Jesus. Father of Mercy, I beg You by the bitter Passion of Your Son and by His three-hour agony on the Cross: Let them, too, glorify the abyss of Your mercy. Amen.

*To understand who are the souls designated for this day, and who in the Diary are called 'lukewarm,' but are also compared to ice and to corpses, we would do well to take note of the definition that the Savior Himself gave to them when speaking to St. Faustina

*about them on one occasion: **There are souls who thwart My efforts** (1682). **Souls without love or devotion, souls full of egoism and selfishness, proud and arrogant souls full of deceit and hypocrisy, lukewarm souls who have just enough warmth to keep themselves alive: My Heart cannot bear this. All the graces that I pour out upon them flow off them as off the face of a rock. I cannot stand them because they are neither good nor bad** (1702).*

Three O'clock Hour Prayer

You expired, Jesus, but the source of life gushed forth for souls, and the ocean of mercy opened up for the whole world. O Fount of Life, unfathomable Divine Mercy, envelop the whole world and empty Yourself out upon us. ... O Blood and Water, which gushed forth from the Heart of Jesus as a fount of mercy for us, I trust in You (*Diary* 1319, 187).

St. Thérèse's Offering to Merciful Love
(Short Version)

O my God! Will Your Justice alone find souls willing to immolate themselves as victims? Does not Your *Merciful Love* need them too? On every side this love is unknown, rejected; those hearts upon whom You would lavish it turn to creatures ... [T]hey do this instead of throwing themselves into Your arms and of accepting Your infinite *Love*. O my God! Is Your disdained Love going to remain closed up within Your Heart? It seems to me that if You were to find souls offering themselves as victims of holocaust to Your Love, You would consume them rapidly; it seems to me, too, that You would be happy not to hold back the waves of infinite tenderness within You. If Your Justice loves to release itself, this Justice *which extends only over the earth*, how much more does Your Merciful Love desire to set souls on fire since Your Mercy *reaches to the heavens*. O my Jesus, let me be this happy victim; consume Your holocaust with the fire of Your Divine Love! (emphasis in original; *Story of a Soul: The Autobiography of St. Thérèse of Lisieux*, trans. John Clarke, OCD [Washington, DC: The Institute of Carmelite Studies, 1996], pp. 180-181).

St. Thérèse's Offering to Merciful Love
(Long Version)

O My God! Most Blessed Trinity, I desire to *Love* You and make You *Loved*, to work for the glory of Holy Church by saving souls on earth and liberating those suffering in purgatory. I desire to accomplish Your will perfectly and to reach the degree of glory You have prepared for me in Your Kingdom. I desire, in a word, to be a saint, but I feel my helplessness and I beg You, O my God! to be Yourself my *Sanctity*!

Since You loved me so much as to give me Your only Son as my Savior and my Spouse, the infinite treasures of His merits are mine. I offer them to You with gladness, begging You to look upon me only in the Face of Jesus and in His heart burning with *Love*.

I offer You, too, all the merits of the saints (in heaven and on earth), their acts of Love, and those of the holy angels. Finally, I offer You, *O Blessed Trinity*! the Love and merits of the *Blessed Virgin, my dear Mother*. It is to her I abandon my offering, begging her to present it to You. Her Divine Son, my Beloved Spouse, told us in the days of His mortal life: "*Whatsoever you ask the Father in my name he will give it to you!*" I am certain, then, that You will grant my desires; I know, O my God! that *the more You want to give, the more You make us desire*. I feel in my heart immense desires and it is with confidence I ask You to come and take possession of my soul. Ah! I cannot receive Holy Communion as often as I desire, but, Lord, are You not *all powerful*? Remain in me as in a tabernacle and never separate Yourself from Your little victim.

I want to console You for the ingratitude of the wicked, and I beg of You to take away my freedom to displease You. If through weakness I sometimes fall, may Your *Divine Glance* cleanse my soul immediately, consuming all my imperfections like the fire that transforms everything into itself.

I thank You, O my God! for all the graces You have granted me, especially the grace of making me pass through the crucible of suffering. It is with joy I shall contemplate You on the Last Day carrying the scepter of Your Cross. Since You deigned to give me a share in this very precious Cross, I hope in heaven to resemble You and to see shining in my glorified body the sacred stigmata of Your Passion.

After earth's Exile, I hope to go and enjoy You in the Fatherland, but I do not want to lay up merits for heaven. I want to work for Your *Love alone* with the one purpose of pleasing You, consoling Your Sacred Heart, and saving souls who will love You eternally.

In the evening of this life, I shall appear before You with empty hands, for I do not ask You, Lord, to count my works. All our justice is stained in Your eyes. I wish, then, to be clothed in Your own *Justice* and to receive from Your *Love* the eternal possession of *Yourself.* I want no other *Throne*, no other *Crown* but You, my *Beloved*!

Time is nothing in Your eyes, and a single day is like a thousand years. You can, then, in one instant prepare me to appear before You.

In order to live in one single act of perfect Love, I OFFER MYSELF AS A VICTIM OF HOLOCAUST TO YOUR MERCIFUL LOVE, asking You to consume me incessantly, allowing the waves of *infinite tenderness* shut up within You to overflow into my soul, and that thus I may become a *martyr* of Your *Love*, O my God!

May this martyrdom, after having prepared me to appear before You, finally cause me to die and may my soul take its flight without any delay into the eternal embrace of *Your Merciful Love.*

I want, O my Beloved, at each beat of my heart to renew this offering to You an infinite number of times, until the shadows having disappeared I may be able to tell You of my Love in an *Eternal Face to Face!* (emphasis in orginal; ibid., pp. 276-277).

Family Offering to Merciful Love and Divine Mercy Enthronement

(with explanations)

A Family Offering to Merciful Love is basically where a family makes a "mercy deal" with Jesus. In other words, they ask Jesus to pour out on them the rejected mercy other families refuse, and for their part, they strive to accept this rejected mercy and share it with others. In our time, when the family is so much under attack, when, sadly, so many families refuse God's mercy, Jesus' Heart is especially wounded. A Family Offering to Merciful Love is meant to give Jesus the consolation of a family that chooses to receive his rejected merciful love. This doesn't mean the family has to be perfect. In fact, the more imperfect they are, the more Jesus longs to pour out his mercy on them. They simply need to be open to receiving and sharing his merciful love. I suggest the following formula for making a Family Offering to Merciful Love, which begins with Jesus' words to St. Faustina:

> Jesus, you said to St. Faustina: **The flames of mercy are burning me. I desire to pour them out upon human souls. Oh, what pain they cause Me when they do not want to accept them!** (1074). **You, at least, come to Me as often as possible and take these graces they do not want to accept. In this way you will console My Heart. Oh, how indifferent are souls to so much goodness, to so many proofs of love! My Heart drinks only of the ingratitude and forgetfulness of souls living in the world. They**

have time for everything, but they have no time to come to Me for graces (367). My daughter, take the graces that others spurn; take as many as you can carry (454). I want to give myself to souls and to fill them with My love, but few there are who want to accept all the graces My love has intended for them. My grace is not lost; if the soul for whom it was intended does not accept it, another soul takes it (1017).

Lord Jesus, if you want to pour your mercy out on souls, how much more must you desire to pour it out on whole families, especially in our time when so many families reject you. Therefore, we the _____ Family offer ourselves to your merciful love and ask for the graces and mercy that other families refuse. We ask this in order to console your Heart and because we need your mercy. Fill us with your mercy, Lord. Please forgive us our sins, and give us the grace to be merciful to one another in our deeds, words, and prayers. May the rays of mercy that go forth from your Heart reign in our home and in our hearts. Please make our home a place where your mercy can rest and where we, too, can find rest in your mercy. Bless us with your mercy when we leave our home and bless us again when we return. Bless everyone we meet with the mercy you pour into our hearts. Especially bless those who visit our home — may they experience your mercy here.

Mary, Mother of Mercy, help us to faithfully live our Offering to God's Merciful Love. We give ourselves to you and ask you to share with us your Immaculate Heart. Help us to accept your Son's mercy with your own openness of heart at the Annunciation. Help us to be grateful for God's mercy with your own joyful heart at the Visitation. Help us to trust in God's mercy, especially during times of darkness, with your own steadfast faith at Calvary. Finally, Mary, protect and preserve our family in love, so that one day we may rejoice together with you and all the saints in the communion of the eternal Family of Love, Father, Son, and Holy Spirit. Amen.

St. Joseph, pray for us.
St. Faustina, pray for us.
St. Thérèse, pray for us.

I recommend that a family make such an offering on one of their favorite Marian Feasts, on St. Joseph's Feast (March 19), or on one of the "Mercy Feasts" such as the memorial of St. Thérèse of Lisieux (Oct. 1) or St. Faustina (Oct. 5), Divine Mercy Sunday (the second Sunday of Easter) or Trinity Sunday, which is the day St. Thérèse first made her Offering to Merciful Love. I further recommend that the Family Offering be accompanied by a Divine Mercy Enthronement, meaning that the family put up in their home an Image of Divine Mercy (if there isn't one already) and ask Jesus to reign there. An appropriate prayer for such an enthronement is as follows:

Jesus, you said to St. Faustina: **"I am offering people a vessel with which they are to keep coming for graces to the fountain of mercy. That vessel is this image with the signature: 'Jesus, I trust in You'** (327). **By means of this image I shall be granting many graces to souls"** (570).

Lord Jesus, through this image of your mercy, please grant us your grace. Whenever we look at it, help us to remember your love and mercy and fill our hearts with trust. Just as your mercy is depicted in this image as going forth from your pierced Heart, surround our home with the rays of your mercy. May the blood and water that flows forth from your Heart always be upon us! Jesus, we trust in you.

I recommend concluding such a prayer by praying a Divine Mercy Chaplet. Also, it might be a good idea to invite a priest to bless your home and your Image of Divine Mercy.

2. PRAYERS OF CONSECRATION TO MARY

Consoler Consecration to Mary
(shorter version)

Mary, I want to be a saint. I know that you also want me to be a saint and that it's your God-given mission to form me into one. So, Mary, at this moment, on this day, I freely choose to give you my full permission to do your work in me, with your Spouse, the Holy Spirit (*CHJ*, p. 113).

Consoler Consecration to Mary
(longer version)

Today I renew my total consecration to you, Mary, my mother. I give you my whole being so you may lead me to console your Son with the perfect consolation you give to him. From this day forward, dear Jesus, whenever I embrace you, may it be with the arms of Mary. Whenever I kiss you, may it be with the lips of Mary. Whenever I sing to you, praise you, and thank you, may it be with the voice of Mary. Jesus, in short, every time I love you, may it be with the Heart of Mary (*CHJ*, p. 114).

St. Louis de Montfort's Consecration to Mary

I, _____ , a faithless sinner, renew and ratify today in thy hands the vows of my Baptism; I renounce forever Satan, his pomps and works; and I give myself entirely to Jesus Christ, the Incarnate Wisdom, to carry my cross after Him all the days of my life, and to be more faithful to Him than I have ever been before. In the presence of all the heavenly court I choose thee this day for my Mother and Mistress. I deliver and consecrate to thee, as thy slave, my body and soul, my goods, both interior and exterior, and even the value of all my good actions, past, present and future; leaving to thee the entire and full right of disposing of me, and all that belongs to me, without exception, according to thy good pleasure, for the greater glory of God in time and in eternity.

St. Maximilian Kolbe's Consecration to Mary

O Immaculata, Queen of Heaven and earth, refuge of sinners and our most loving Mother, God has willed to entrust the entire order of mercy to you. I, _____, a repentant sinner, cast myself at your feet humbly imploring you to take me with all that I am and have, wholly to yourself as your possession and property. Please make of me, of all my powers of soul and body, of my whole life, death and eternity, whatever most pleases you. If it pleases you, use all that I am and have without reserve, wholly to accomplish what was said of you: "She will crush your head," and, "You alone have destroyed all heresies in the whole world."

Let me be a fit instrument in your immaculate and merciful hands for introducing and increasing your glory to the maximum in all the many strayed and indifferent souls, and thus help extend as far as possible the blessed kingdom of the most Sacred Heart of Jesus. For wherever you enter you obtain the grace of conversion and growth in holiness, since it is through your hands that all graces come to us from the most Sacred Heart of Jesus.

> V. *Allow me to praise you, O Sacred Virgin.*
> R. Give me strength against your enemies.

3. SHORT PRAYERS FROM THE *CONSOLING THE HEART OF JESUS* RETREAT

Yes to Jesus (*CHJ*, p. 33)

Jesus, I thirst for you. Help me to thirst for you more. Use me, Jesus. Form me into a saint. Make up for all my faults. I trust in you. With Mary's help, I give you my yes.

A Bold Prayer (*CHJ*, p. 75)

Father, behold the suffering of your Son, Jesus. I lift him up to you. Although I'm weak and don't have much to offer by myself, dear Father, your Son's merits are infinite. So, behold, to your Son's suffering, I unite my own, and I ask you to save all those poor, unrepentant sinners who have no one else to pray for them. Yes, Father, I believe that your Son's infinite merits can accomplish this.

When My Sin Discourages Me
(*CHJ*, p. 88)

O Jesus, I feel that I've ruined everything by my sin. I'm so sorry for what I've done, and I will do my best not to do it again. Dear Jesus, by the power of your infinite mercy, I trust that somehow you can fix not only the evil I've done but bring an even greater good out of it.

For Uniting My Will to God's Will
(*CHJ*, p. 90)

Jesus, behold, I give you my heart. If my desires aren't in harmony with yours, then please change them according to your wisdom and love. Dear Jesus, you know that by myself, I'm too weak to change my desires, but you can do it. Jesus, I trust you to do it. Jesus, I thank you in advance for doing it.

Prayer before a Crucifix (*CHJ*, p. 102)

Lord Jesus, even though my sins are many, I know the mercy of your Heart. I'm sorry I was afraid to go to you. I'm so sorry I left you alone. But look, here I am. Please forgive me my sins. I'm going to try to do better. Lord, I can't offer much right now except for my weak trust and love. Jesus, I do trust in you, and I love you. Praise you, Jesus, and thank you for everything, especially for what you're suffering right now out of love for me. I've come to be with you, my friend. Don't be sad. I love you, and there's nowhere else I'd rather be than right here, praising you, thanking you, and consoling your broken Heart.

Modified Breathing Prayer "Deal"
(*CHJ*, p. 164)

Lord, you can understand people in any language, including sign language. Well, I'd like to translate the "O Blood and Water" prayer into sign language. So, Lord, I propose the following deal. Anytime I consciously inhale with the intention of receiving the blood and water that gushed forth from your pierced side, I ask you to fill me with your merciful love. Then, when I exhale with the intention of giving this mercy to others, I ask you to give them the grace of the "O Blood and Water" prayer, namely, the grace of conversion. (For the "O Blood and Water" prayer, see p. 105 or *Diary*, 187.)

Surrender of Worries (*CHJ*, p. 171)

O Jesus, I surrender this to you. You take care of it.

(This prayer is attributed to St. Padre Pio's spiritual director, Dom Dolindo Ruotolo. It is said that to this priest Jesus promised that whoever would surrender his worries, difficulties, and problems to Jesus with the words of this prayer, Jesus would take special, even miraculous care of what is surrendered to him.)

B. PLAN OF LIFE

"Behold this Heart which loves so much
yet is so little loved."

Consoler Principle and Foundation

I_____, on this
day _____ , choose as my principle
and foundation to console the Heart of Jesus.

Dear Jesus, relying on your grace and the
prayers of Mary and of all the angels and saints,
I will strive to keep before my eyes the deep
sorrow of your Heart and respond, with Mary,
by consoling you in the following two ways:

First, I will give you my trust. Jesus, I
trust in you. I will try not to be afraid of going
to you as I am (*ecce*), even when my sins and
weaknesses weigh heavily upon me. With an
open heart, I choose to accept your mercy
(*fiat*), even all that mercy other souls reject.
Finally, I will do my best to praise and thank
you in all things (*magnificat*), even when you
give me the privilege of sharing in your Cross.

Second, I will strive to show mercy to my
neighbor through my deeds, words, and
prayers, remembering that by consoling others,
I am also consoling you.

Heavenly Father, for the sake of the
sorrowful Passion of your Son, I beg you:
Send forth your Holy Spirit to help me fulfill
this choice.

A Consoler's Three Promises

1. I will live my principle and foundation of consoling Jesus, with Mary, by giving him my trust (see "A Summary of Trust" on next page) and by doing acts of mercy according to the following three degrees:

    (a) Deed — especially the merciful outlook

    (b) Word — especially the merciful question

    (c) Prayer — especially the Chaplet of Divine Mercy and "breathing prayer"

2. I will keep to a simple schedule of daily prayer:

    (a) Morning Offering (see pp. 123-124)

    (b) Three O'clock Hour (see p. 124)

    (c) Examination of Conscience: B-A-K-E-R (see p. 126)

3. I will frequent the Sacraments and take time for spiritual reading.

I will frequent the Sacraments by going to Mass every Sunday and maybe even during the week. I will go to confession at least once a year and maybe even once or twice a month. I will consider visiting Jesus in the Blessed Sacrament more regularly, and I will strive to visit him frequently in the tabernacle of my heart.

A Summary of Trust: *Ecce, Fiat, Magnificat*

1. *Ecce* = "Behold." Behold, Lord, here I am, weaknesses, sinfulness and all.

2. *Fiat* = "Let it be done to me." Lord Jesus, pour out the ocean of your mercy into the abyss of my misery. I choose to accept your mercy, even the mercy that others refuse.

3. *Magnificat* = "My soul proclaims the greatness of the Lord!" I praise and thank you, Lord Jesus, for the great gift of your mercy and for all your gifts, including my small sharing in your Cross.

Morning Offering

Dear Jesus, I know that your Sacred Heart is sorrowful because so many people neither love you nor trust in you. Behold, Lord, here I am. Though weak and sinful, I love you and I trust in you. I intend that all my actions this day be for the purpose of consoling you.

Heavenly Father, in union with all the Masses being offered today, I give you praise and thanks for the many gifts you will send me, including the gift of my small sharing in the Cross. May this my prayer glorify you and console your Son. With the help of your grace,

I resolve to remain all day in this prayerful spirit of praise and thanks and, further, to console Jesus by being merciful to my neighbor through my deeds, words, and prayers.

Mary, my mother, come with your spouse, the Spirit. Make my sacrifice of praise, thanks, and mercy a most pleasing consolation to your Son. Behold, I present to you all I am and have. Take my offering so it may pass through your Immaculate Heart, to Jesus' Sacred Heart, and on to the Father, for his greater glory. Amen.

Three Ways to Keep the Three O'clock Hour

1. We can *immerse ourselves in the Lord's Passion, especially in his abandonment on the Cross.* We can do this briefly (even "for an instant") or for a longer period of time. For example, we can simply look at a crucifix, think of Jesus in his Passion, or pray the Three O'clock Hour Prayer:

> You expired, Jesus, but the source of life gushed forth for souls, and the ocean of mercy opened up for the whole world. O Fount of Life, unfathomable Divine Mercy, envelop the whole world and empty Yourself out upon us. ... O Blood and Water, which gushed forth from the Heart of Jesus as a fount of mercy for us, I trust in You (*Diary*, 1319, 187).

If we have more time, we can pray the sorrowful mysteries of the Rosary or make the Stations of the Cross. Here is a map for busy people who want to make the stations over the course of two weeks:

Sunday	Monday	Tuesday	Wednesday	Thursday	Friday	Saturday
I. Jesus is condemned to death.	II. Jesus takes up his Cross.	III. Jesus falls the first time.	IV. Jesus meets his blessed mother.	V. Simon of Cyrene helps Jesus to carry the Cross.	VI. Veronica wipes the face of Jesus.	VII. Jesus falls a second time.

Sunday	Monday	Tuesday	Wednesday	Thursday	Friday	Saturday
VIII. Jesus consoles the women of Jerusalem.	IX. Jesus falls the third time.	X. Jesus is stripped of his garments.	XI. Jesus is nailed to the Cross.	XII. Jesus dies on the Cross.	XIII. Jesus is laid in the arms of his blessed mother.	XIV. Jesus is laid in the tomb.

2. We can *present our petitions to the Father by virtue of his Son's Passion*. Our petitions should be made with bold confidence because of the indescribable power of Jesus' Passion and the great promises attached to the Hour of Great Mercy. I recommend presenting one's petitions in the context of praying the Divine Mercy Chaplet. (Don't forget to pray for unrepentant sinners and the dying, especially for unrepentant sinners who are dying.)

3. The three o'clock hour is a great time to visit Jesus, truly present in the Blessed Sacrament.

Examination of Conscience: B-A-K-E-R

(Begin by putting yourself in the presence of God.)

B = Blessings. Spend the most time here, praising and thanking God for the blessings of the day.

A = Ask. Ask the Holy Spirit to enlighten you, so you can recognize your sins.

K = Kill. It was our sins that killed and crucified Jesus. Search for commissions and omissions.

E = Embrace. Be sorry for sin and allow Jesus to embrace you with the rays of his mercy.

R = Resolution. Look ahead to the next day, anticipating potential pitfalls and opportunities.

For a more extensive treatment of the preceding Plan of Life, see the Conclusion to *CHJ*, pp. 169-195 and the corresponding References and Notes, pp. 417-426. Also, Consolers may want to enhance their Plan of Life by studying the Rules for the Discernment of Spirits (for Little Souls) that comprises Appendix One of *CHJ*, pp. 199-252.

Continue your experience
with *Consoling the Heart of Jesus.*

➤ Download the Free Divine Mercy App, featuring an Interactive Chaplet.

➤ Join the *Consoling the Heart of Jesus* group on Facebook.

➤ Visit thedivinemercy.org/chj

  • Download the Consoler Cheat Sheet and other prayers related to the retreat.

  • Join the *Confraternity of Consolers,* a spiritual benefit society.

  • Purchase additional copies of the *Prayer Companion* and *Consoling the Heart of Jesus* for family and friends.

➤ Ask about Hearts Afire: Parish-based Programs from the Marian Fathers of the Immaculate Conception (HAPP®), featuring *Consoling the Heart of Jesus* and *33 Days to Morning Glory.* Visit AllHeartsAfire.org or call 877-200-4277.

CHJ   **PCCHJ**   **33DAY**

If you don't have internet access and would like to purchase additional copies of *Consoling the Heart of Jesus,* please call 1-800-462-7426. Also, for Marian Press's complete line of DVDs, books, and more, visit marian.org/giftshop or call the number above to have the latest catalog sent to you.